Chief Executive Author

The Business Building Guide for Book Writers

By Vanessa Collins, CDMP

Heart Thoughts Publishing
Floyds Knobs, IN

Printed in the United States of America

ISBN: 9781709169885

Heart Thoughts Publishing
P.O. Box 536
Floyds Knobs, IN 47119
www.HeartThoughtsPublishing.com
Vanessa@HeartThoughtsPublishing.com

Dedication

To my business besties. Thank you for all that you do.

Thank You...

for purchasing this book. As my gift to you, please visit
ChiefExecutiveAuthor.com/BookBonuses
get access to our FREE Online Resource Page that has
exclusive videos training, worksheets and other
resources designed specifically for this book.

Also, don't forget to leave a review on Amazon.

Table of Contents

Introduction

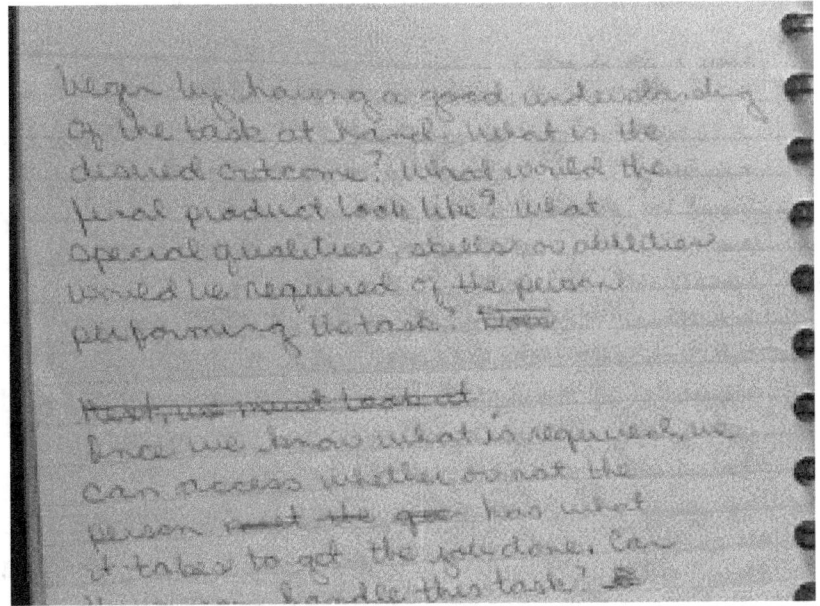

*T*his is how my first book started out. It was a handwritten devotional that I was planning to teach for a Bible class. It was filled with terrible handwriting and bad grammar, but I knew what I wanted to say. Putting it on paper got the thoughts out of my head so that I could refine them. That was 1998.

Fast forward ten years later to 2008. I was searching on the internet for a book. I found the book on a site called Lulu.com. Once I placed the order, I received a confirmation screen indicating my book would be shipped as soon as it was printed. Printed? I looked at the copyright date which showed the book was over ten years old. This was NOT a new book. Why would it need to be printed?

That day I discovered something which would forever change my life, on-demand printing. I always wanted to publish a book, but in 1998 there was no such thing as self-publishing. Even by 2001, the cost to have a vanity publisher produce a book started at $5000. However, I was able to publish my first book in 2009 for the whopping price of $35, which was the cost of the three proof copies I ordered because I wanted to make sure "it was real" before I spent the time putting the book together. It was real. My journey as an author, and eventually a publisher, began.

Since then, I have written six books. Between the two publishing companies I helped start and my coaching firm, I have helped over 50 authors with over 100 books. It started with one thing, THAT FIRST BOOK.

That first book, Intensive Faith Therapy, when on to birth a ministry, two publishing companies, a coaching firm, four conferences, and some online products and services, earning well into five figures. However, it took me over four years to break that $10,000 mark with my first book because I didn't know the things I am going to share with you in this book. With my last book, Digital Mastery for Women, it took less than six months to break the $10,000 barrier, and the services produced from that book are generating over $1,000 every month.

I have talked to a number of authors over the years, and they all have one concern; how do they generate more revenue from their book. Many of them think more revenue is going to come from selling more books. While you will make more money as you sell more books, selling more books is not the key to generating substantial revenue from your book. I'm sorry. I don't mean the burst your bubble.

Yes, you could sell $10,000 worth of books. That would require you sell 500 to 1000 books, depending on what you charge. Let's be honest, most of us have never sold 1000 anything before. While it is possible, it may not be the best way to get to your goal.

My goal is to help you get to your goal. From my experience, the best way you help you achieve your goal is to empower you with the information you need so you can develop a profitable strategy for your book. That is going to require you become familiar with two things: digital marketing and product creation.

This book is going to help authors who have no digital marketing experience, create products based on their books. Even if you have experience in digital marketing, I am sure you will find some nuggets here which will take your business to the next level.

I have shared a ton of information in this book, probably too much (I know a few of my coaches will think so). But my goal is that you can use this as a reference book as you do your next book project. If it seems like it is a lot of work, it is. I won't lie and try to sugar coat it. I wish there were a shortcut. There is not. It will take work. But I can promise you this. It will be some of the most rewarding work you have ever done.

Chapter 1 – Why Chief Executive Author?

*W*hen you think about a Chief Executive Officer (CEO), you imagine the head of a corporation. This is the person in charge; the big boss, so to speak. According to an article by Tom Lin, the Chief Executive Officer is charged with maximizing the value of the entity[i].

As an author, you are the Chief Executive Officer for the entity you have created, your book. Just as corporate CEOs are responsible for making sure the products and services offered by their companies maximize profits, the author is responsible for the same. As an author, you are in charge. You determine how successfully your book will be. Unfortunately, most authors do not have the resources corporate CEOs have. However, that does not relieve you, as the author, of this responsibility. You must make your book successful.

You can be an author who sells a few books at vendor events, or you can be a Chief Executive Author (CEA) who touches and changes lives through the powerful messages you deliver in your books and other products and services. Being a CEA is about having passion and getting your life-changing message to the world. But it's more than just getting the message out there. It's about equipping and empowering your reader to be able to manifest the changes they so desperately desire. You are not just an information pusher. You are an implementor, and you help your readers implement changes in their lives. You are truly a life-changer.

The Bottom Line of Business

There are many elements required to make a corporation successful, especially in this age of digital marketing. However, most authors who do not have other entrepreneurial experiences don't understand digital marketing and how that impacts the bottom line of business.

First, let's get clear on what the bottom line of business is, especially for an author. The bottom line of business is straightforward. You must get your products and services into the hands of your customers. For an author that means getting your book into the hands of your potential readers. In exchange for your products and services (or books), your customers (or readers) will give you some sort of compensation. That may be in the form of money, reviews or even their e-mail addresses. All three of these are essential.

How do you get your books into the hands of your customers? There are five critical things you need to do to make this happen. Everything you do to market your book should support at least one of these objectives.

You must:

- Find your readers or make it easy for them to find you.

- Find out what your readers want or need.

- Inform, educate and convince your readers that your book can meet their needs.

- Deliver your book in a way that suits your readers.

- Have systems in place to receive compensation. That compensation may be in the form of currency, reviews or an email address.

Don't Play Hide and Seek - Let Readers Find You

Having a great message in your book is awesome. However, if no one reads that book because they can't find that book, it isn't helpful. Your potential reader must be able to find you. Although this may seem like a "no-brainer," you may be surprised how many authors miss this. Perhaps you are not surprised. Maybe you have had the experience of looking for a book but not being able to find it. You may have searched on Amazon, or tried to find the author's website, but to no avail. So, you ended up finding another book or just going without. As an author, especially a Chief Executive Author, your digital marketing strategy must include helping your readers find you. This includes your website and social media presence.

It's Really Not About You – Find Out What Your Readers Want/Need

This is a cornerstone of business philosophy many have forgotten. We often try to put the proverbial cart before the horse on this one. We may feel inspired to write a book about our lives or experiences. After we spend countless hours poring over our words, trying to make sure every punctuation is in place, we present our book to the world. This is more than a book. It is our baby. It contains some of our deepest thoughts and well-kept secrets. We have poured our hearts into the pages. We announce to the world that our new baby has been born and we present our latest creation to the masses. We make announcements on social media or flood the inboxes of our family and friends with invitations to partake of this mighty offering (i.e., buy our book). Then we discover the unthinkable; no one is jumping to buy.

> You can be an author who sells a few books at vendor events, or you can be a Chief Executive Author (CEA) who touches and changes lives through the powerful messages you deliver in your books and other products and services.

Often as authors, we forget an important product creation fact and that is that our book needs to solve a problem or meet the needs of our reader. Do you know what problem your book solves? Even if it is a work of fiction that is designed to entertain, it is still solving a problem. It is combating boredom in someone's life.

Once you know what problem you solve, you must be able to articulate that in a way that resonates with your potential reader. Your book may have solved a significant problem and answered a huge question, but we must find the readers who have that significant problem or need an answer to that huge question. We often write from such a personal point of view that we don't articulate clearly how our message will impact and change our reader's life.

Help Me Help You - Inform, Educate and Convince

Once you know who your readers are and what they need, you must inform, educate and convince them that your book can meet their needs. While this may seem easy enough, many of us fail to do this. Often, authors have people in their sphere of influence who have no idea they have written a book or have a program that can solve their problem. You don't want to constantly hear from the people around you, "I didn't know you wrote a book about that subject." Being the best kept secret in business is NOT good.

There are several things you can do to prevent this.

- Make sure your social media profiles are complete and comprehensive. Some social media profiles like LinkedIn rank very high in search results.

- Make sure your profile contains the keywords your customers are searching on and don't forget to list your books. For keyword research, use a tool like Google Planner, formerly known as Google Keyword Tool. Although this tool is part of the Google Adwords site, you do not need to purchase an Adwords campaign to use the tool.

- Make sure you update your website often with your latest products and services. Schedule a time once a quarter to review your social media profiles and websites.

Sometimes you will find you need to educate your potential readers on what they need. They may understand the problem they are having but not know what solutions are available to them. This is a case of "not knowing" what you don't know. Once you have informed your potential reader of what you can do for them and possibly even educated them on a solution, you must convince them your book is the right book for them. It's a simple question. Why should they read your book? You must craft an

If you are doing activities that do not support the bottom line of your business, you are wasting valuable time.

articulate answer to this question. This is old-fashioned marketing, at its finest.

Have It Your Way – Deliver Your Book in A Way Your Readers Want

I grew up during the time where there were encyclopedia salespeople. These people would go door to door selling sets of these wonderful books. If you could afford a set of encyclopedias, which could cost several hundreds of dollars, your family was doing well, especially where I lived.

Then a funny thing happened. Personal computers were born. As personal computers advanced, the type of data they could display advanced. I remember getting my first CD that contained the entire encyclopedia on it. I stared at the disc in amazement. If an encyclopedia salesman had knocked on my door at that very moment, they would have been very unhappy.

In this technology age, many people prefer content delivered in a digital format. You must make sure to include this in your offerings. For instance, as an author, you should consider having your book available not only in print form but also in eBook and audiobook format, especially if that is the way your customer prefers the content. You will notice many top-selling business books are available in eBook and audiobook formats because many business executives like to listen to content on their tablets and smartphones. Here, again, it is important to know your customer. Do your customers like to get your type of information in digital format? If so, make sure you can deliver it that way.

Show Me the Money - Receiving Compensation

One would think having systems in place to receive compensation would be the easiest thing in the world. But it isn't, and you know this from experience.

Have you ever attempted to make a purchase all to find out the business does not accept the type of currency you have available to you at that moment? It is frustrating and, unfortunately, it is the death of many sales. Remember, we must not only be able to deliver the product/service into our customer's hands, but we must also be able to receive some type of compensation for it.

At a minimum, you must have a system like PayPal or something like accept payments from customers. You must be able to accept credit cards payments securely. Many shopping cart services will allow you to offer convenient and safe payment processing for your customers. However, at live events, make sure you have plenty of change as well. Many people use cash, and it is very frustrating for potential readers when attempting to make a purchase, to find out the author can't make change for the purchase.

Other Forms of "Payment"

Remember, currency is not the only compensation you need to be able to accept. Sometimes you need to expand your mailing list and generate leads. You may do this with what is known as a "lead magnet." We will discuss lead magnets more in another chapter. However, to offer a lead magnet, you need to have a system in place to accept email addresses. You will also need an autoresponder in place to deliver the content once they sign up for it.

Each of the aspects of digital marketing we will discuss in this book is designed to support one or more of these areas. If you are doing activities that do not support the bottom line of your business, you are wasting valuable time.

Chapter 2 – Write Your Book FAST

*L*et's not move too fast here. To be a Chief Executive Author, you need to have a book. That's simple enough. Writing a book is not difficult, but it does take time and dedication. But the time and dedication will all be worth it. If you already have a book, feel free to skip to Section 2 but let me warn you, I have some great tips in these next few chapters will help you write, publish and promote your next book faster and increase profitably. But, if you are in a hurry, go ahead. We'll be here.

As a speaker, coach or entrepreneur, you often motivate and encourage with your words. You inspire people to make life-changing decisions and take bold action steps to accomplish their goals and live their dreams. But when the speech is over, only the memory of the spoken words remains. Unfortunately, as the days and weeks go by, those memories fade. However, if your audience was able to experience your words again, in greater detail, it would be a huge benefit for them and would increase their chances of success immensely.

There are also tremendous benefits for you to have your work published as well. It is no secret having a book increases your credibility with your audience as well as your bottom line. At live events, many authors make substantially more from their book sales than they do with the speaker's honorarium. It is a sad, but true, fact. As a speaker, you are leaving money on the table when you do not have books and other products to sell. Leaving money on the table is a big "no-no" for Chief Executive Authors.

Writing a book is not hard at all, but it does require work. If you are like many of my clients, you have already written your book several times in your head. Now the

No lives will be changed by the book that is stuck in your head.

goal is the get that masterpiece out of your head and on to paper. Remember, your number one focus is to change people's lives. No lives will be changed by the book that is stuck in your head. You must get your message out to those who need it.

In my many years of teaching the Write Your Book FAST™ boot camp, I have found the following process will make your book writing challenge easier.

- Research How to Write a Book
- Decide Your Topic
- Research Your Topic
- Decide Your Hook
- Outline Your Book

- Write the Actual Draft
- Craft the Second Draft

Let's look at each of these elements a little closer.

Research How to Write a Book

How you write a novel is different than how you write a non-fiction book. Spend a few days looking at what it will take to write your book. There are several excellent books out there on this subject, and my goal is not to reinvent the wheel. In addition to the tips in this chapter, I suggest you look at the following books. At the time of this writing, each of these books is available on Amazon® in Kindle® format. Remember, you do not need a Kindle® device to read a Kindle® book. You can download the Kindle® app for your PC, smartphone or tablet.

How to Write a Nonfiction eBook in 21 Days - That Readers LOVE! By Steve Scott

Write Compelling Fiction by L. J. Martin

How to Write a Fiction Novel in 30 Days Nicholas Black

Decide Your Topic

If you are like most people, you have some books swimming around in your head, waiting to get out. Choose 1 and complete that. It's doesn't mean you won't complete the other books. To the contrary, completing the first book increases the likelihood you will complete the others. However, if you spend too much time trying to figure out which book to write first, you won't write any.

Make a list of all the books you would like to write. As an entrepreneur, you should have a book on every major topic you cover. If you are a speaker, you should have a book on each of your signature presentations. Having a book on the topic you speak on will increase your sales tremendously at speaking events, but we will cover that topic later. If you are a minister, you should have a book on your popular sermon or teaching series.

Once you have your list, pick the top 3 books you would like to complete in the next 12 months. Here are some criteria you can use in choosing your top 3 books.

- Which books do you have the most information on at this present moment?

- Which books have you started already?

- If you have started writing, which books are the closest to being completed?

- Which books would align with the major classes or programs you are launching in the next six months?

Now that you have your top 3, it's time to decide on one. Pick one! Make a decision. Don't procrastinate and don't over think it. In my writer's boot camp, I give participants 1 week to make this decision. I offer this same to you. If you haven't chosen your book already, I am giving you a week. ☺ Mark your calendar a week from today and make sure you make your decision by then. If you would like for me to help you be accountable, join my <u>Digital Mastery For Authors Facebook Group</u>[ii] (it's free) and post in the group. My team would love to help keep you accountable.

Research Your Topic

If you are writing a non-fiction book about a subject you are not an expert on, spend about a week researching your topic. I suggest you look at least three of the top books on your subject and read blog posts from the last 60 days from the top six blogs on your subject. The books will provide an overview of your topic and give you a sense of what people agree and disagree on within the realm of your topic. The blogs or articles will provide you with a sense of what's new and hot in your area. While I don't think you need to read three books on your subject completely, you should read the sections of the book that are relevant to your specific topic. I also suggest you look up at least three industry leaders in your field and see what articles or interviews they have published in the last year.

Along with researching the content for your book, you need to research the market for your book. Look for the top 3 books that talk about your subject matter. If, in the unlikely event, there are no books on your subject matter, make sure there is a market for your book. While you may have a passion for underwater basket weaving, there may not be a market for it. Many other coaches would tell you at this point you should reject this book idea and move on to another book idea that is more marketable. I am not going to say that. If you are passionate about the subject, I encourage you to write the book anyway. However, understand you may have to get creative when it comes to marketing your book.

Why write it if there is not a defined market to sell it to? I believe when you stop writing the book of your passion, you dampen your creativity. The more you write, the more ideas come. When you have a burning idea for a book, and you don't take the time to write it, it hampers other ideas from flowing. If you feel truly passionate and driven to write a particular book then write it. Once you have gotten those ideas out of your head, you allow room for other ideas to blossom. It could be one of those ideas that become a best seller.

Amazon reviews are a goldmine of marketing information about your subject and audience needs and preferences. Look at the Amazon reviews for the top 3 to 5 books on your subject material. Read the positive reviews. What are some of the things your audience is looking for in this type of book? What are some of the positive aspects of the book they mentioned? Also, look at the negative comments. This is where you can really get an understanding of your audience's mindset. What are some of the things they didn't like about the book? What are some of the things they were looking for in the book that the author didn't deliver? This is an excellent opportunity to learn what your target audience is looking for in this type of book. Remember, these are probably some of the same people who will be interested in your book.

Decide Your Hook

What is the main idea you want people to walk away with once they have read your book? That's the hook. Once you have decided this, you will have a good idea of where you want to take your audience. Completing this step will help you not to ramble in your book. Many authors have trouble figuring out how to end the book or "land the plane" as Julia Royston says.

If you are writing a fiction book, figure out how the book will end BEFORE you start writing it. Even if you decide to change it once you have started, you at least have an idea of what direction you are heading in when you start. It is like taking a trip in your car using a GPS. You must put the destination in the GPS before you take off. That way, you know, at least, which direction to head in. As with driving, you may see something that catches your eye, and you may stop and check it out. That's fine. But once that pit stop is over, you can get back in the car and continue in the direction of your destination.

Outline Your Book

Once you have decided what the main hook is, what are the 8, 10 or 12 ideas the reader needs to get on that hook? Those become your chapters titles.

If you are writing a non-fiction book, you will want to start with a good outline. There are several ways to do this. You can do an old fashion outline where you list your major topics with subtopics under each. You can use an index card system where you write a major heading on each card and then write subtopics on the back. If you are more technologically inclined, you can use a mind map to outline your subject. There are some great resources in the appendix to do this.

I like the system described in the book, "How to Write a Nonfiction eBook in 21 Days - That Readers LOVE!" Steve Scott suggests you start with your research notes and then do what he calls a "brain dump." Write down every idea you have for your book. Don't worry about organization at this point, just write.

Once you have completed this step, use index cards to organize your thoughts into chapters. Use one index card for each chapter. Write the main idea you want to present in that chapter on one side of the card. On the other side, write down the subtopics for that chapter. Repeat that for each chapter in your book.

You can also accomplish this electronically through Word or other programs like Scrivener, which is designed especially for authors. In Word, I will typically list out my working chapter titles. I make them "Heading 1" under the styles section. To do this, highlight the title, make sure you are in the "Home" tab and click "Heading 1" in the style section. I then write my subtitles underneath.

If you are writing a fiction book, make sure you download my Rough Draft Planning Tool which will help you produce your character sketches, outline your setting, plot and your climax. You will find that on the resource page at ChiefExecutiveAuthor.com.

When I participated in the National Novel Writing Month's challenge to write a 50,000-word novel in 30 days, I started with an outline of the scenes I wanted to have in the book. I envisioned it as a movie. As I told myself the about the "movie," I jotted down the particular scenes. This became my guide for writing the book.

If you want to explore other ways to outline your fiction book, I strongly suggest doing the exercises described in Nicholas Black's book, "How to Write a Fiction Novel in 30 Days."

Write the Actual Draft

Now it's time to write. If you have outlined your book as suggested, writing the rough draft will not be difficult. Simply go through your outline, pick a section and start writing. Do not edit, just write. I find it easier to type my writing as I am doing it. If you decide to handwrite it first, that is fine.

Here is where the commitment comes in. You must commit to writing. You must set aside some time to write. You decide your schedule. Maybe you have decided to write every day or every other day. Whatever your schedule, do it.

You may want to use some type of timing system when you write. Many writers use the Pomodoro Technique developed by Francesco Cirillo. With this technique, you write in 25-minute intervals with 5-minute breaks.

Here are a few tips I use during this rough draft phase.

- Don't worry about writing the chapters in order.

- Do not re-read what you have written. No editing allowed during this phase.

- Always keep a notebook or a few blank index cards with you. If an idea comes, write it down. If you are not able to write, use your phone to record a voice memo to yourself.

- Do not stop to research a topic during your writing time. Make yourself a quick note to do it later if you are afraid you will forget.

- Resist the urge to tear up or delete something. If you decide to go in a different direction, start a new paragraph and write as if the first one did not exist. You may find during your editing process you can use ideas from both.

- If you are stuck on a certain section, skip it and come back later.

Try to pace yourself during this phase. In my writing boot camps, I suggest you commit to writing five hours a week. If you have a traditional schedule where you work 40 hours a week and are off on the weekends, I suggest you choose three weekdays you can write for 1 hour. You can break it up into two ½ hour sessions. Then select a weekend day you can write for two hours. Although everyone's writing speed is different, you may find it takes you about two hours of writing time to complete a chapter. If you are consistent with the five hours per week, you should be able to complete about 2 ½ chapters per week. For a 10-chapter book, you can finish the rough draft in as little as four weeks.

Craft the Second Draft

If you followed my instructions and wrote your rough draft without editing, it probably looks like a hot mess. That's okay. You have accomplished the goal of the rough draft, and that is to get the book out of your head and on paper. Congrats!

Now that you have completed the first draft, it is time to do the heavy editing and rewriting. You may find that your rough draft is not as bad as you may have thought. Or, you may find that you have great content, but the flow and organization need help. In any case, here is where the hard work begins.

> Do not share your project with those who do not believe in you and will say things to discourage you.

Once again, I refer you to "<u>How to Write a Nonfiction eBook in 21 Days - That Readers LOVE!</u>" by Steve Scott. His chapter on "The Art of an Excellent Second Draft" is great.

Following are some of the steps I use when crafting my second draft.

Type Manuscript

If you have not already, it is time to type your manuscript in whatever word processing program you have chosen. I recommend Microsoft® Word because it is easy to format your manuscript for print. However, I have used Microsoft Word for years, so I may be a little biased. As you are typing, you will probably find corrections that need to be made. Go ahead and make those corrections.

Organize the Chapters

Figure out what order you want your content presented and move things around as you need to. Make sure that you save your manuscript often. I cannot stress this enough. Save it on your computer. Save it to a cloud-based program like OneDrive or Dropbox. Save it on a flash drive. Email it to yourself. I don't suggest that you do 1 of these, I suggest that you do ALL of these.

Initial Spell Check Run

I usually run spell check as soon as I have finished typing my rough draft. You will probably have to run it a few times as you make changes. I like to make this initial run so that I am not distracted by obvious misspellings.

Read and Correct

Read your rough draft carefully and made the corrections as needed. Make sure that you check for the following:

- Are complete sentences used, meaning that each sentence has a subject and predicate?

- Do all sentences begin with a capital letter?

- Do all proper nouns begin with capital letters?

- Are periods and commas used correctly?

- Are quotations punctuated correctly?

- Are apostrophes used correctly?

- Do all main verbs agree with the subject in person and number?

- Are any parts of verb phrases missing or incorrect?

- Are verb endings correct?

- Is the verb tense correct?

- Are helping verbs used when needed?

- Do regular plurals end in "s"?

- Are irregular plurals correct?

- Are articles "a," "an," and "the" used correctly?

- Does every pronoun have a clear referent?

- Are words spelled correctly? (Be careful of words that sound the same but have different meanings.)

- Are words used that give a picture of what is taking place?

- Are transitional words used?

- Do sentences begin with different words?

Although you will probably submit your manuscript to an editor, you want to present the best draft possible. Also, the more corrections an editor must make, the more they will probably charge.

Enhance Your Writing

Are there things you need to add to enhance your writing? Perhaps an example or an illustration will help clarify certain sections. Also, make sure that you go back and research those areas that may have come up while you were writing your rough draft. Add any citations or references that are needed. You want to make sure to give proper credit to other authors if you quoted their work.

Stay Motivated

This phase is probably the hardest phase in this whole process. Stay motivated and encouraged. You have put a lot of work into your project and now is not the time to quit. If you feel a little down or overwhelmed, make sure that you reach out for help.

Input from Others

This can be very tricky. At this point, it is probably a good idea to let someone who you trust read over your manuscript before you send it to the editor. However, make sure that it is trustworthy and encouraging. Do not share your project with those who do not believe in you and will say things to discourage you. You know who those people are. This is not the time for them to see it and you do not have anything to prove to anyone.

Chapter 3 - Turn Your Speech or Sermon into a Book

*I*f you are a speaker or a minister, you will want to consider turning your signature presentations or sermons into a book. If you have written a speech, you have a lot of the hard work already done when it comes to writing your book. You already decided a topic and thoroughly researched it before you wrote your speech. You probably cut some valuable information out of the speech to make it shorter so that you could meet your time requirements. It's time to gather all of that material up and start writing your book. Here are some tips that you can use to turn your speech or sermon into a book.

Start with The Outline

If you typically outline your speeches/sermons before you write them, that is the place to start. If you do not outline your speech before writing it, you can go back and outline it. Outlining your speech will help you organize the thoughts that you have and help you decide how to expand. In a typical 20-30-minute speech, you may have 4 – 6 points that you cover. You will probably want to expand this to 8 -10 for your book. Each of the subtopics can be a chapter in your book.

Expand Your Outline

Look at your current outline to see how you can expand it. This is where you can recover the information you previously discarded when you were editing your speech for time. If in your speech you talked about five tips for doing something, see if you can come up with five additional tips for a total of ten tips.

Expand Your Writing

Now it's time to write the chapters for the subtopics in your outline. If you talked about the subtopic in your speech, start there and expand on what you already covered. Otherwise, begin writing on one of the new subtopics. You can also expand your writing by including some of the following elements:

- Etymology / Word Use
- Historical Context
- Geographical Context
- Personal Stories
- Other's stories
- Current /Recent Past Events
- Expert Opinions
- Opposing Views

Etymology

Etymology is the study of the origin of words and the way in which their meanings have changed throughout history. This can be critical when it comes to explaining passages of scripture because the original text was written in Greek and Hebrew. This is also useful when looking at popular English translations like the King James Version, which was translated over 400 years ago. There are some online tools you can use, although I still love my print copies of the Strong's Concordance, Vine's Expository Dictionary and Greek/Hebrew Lexicon.

Various Translations

You may want to reference different translations of the scriptures you use. Always make sure that you state the version you are referring to. Also, make sure that you understand the pros and cons of the version you use and be careful of portions of scripture that were not found in early manuscripts. Be mindful of how you refer to italicized words in the King James Version since the translators added those words.

Historical Context

Are there historical perspectives that are not apparent today? You can also explore how language, people, and culture affected the narrative you are explaining. For instance, when discussing the teachings of Jesus, it is always interesting to note the different groups of people that would interact with His message. The Sadducees, who didn't believe in the resurrection reacted differently to His teachings than the Pharisees, who did believe in resurrection.

Geographical Context

What landforms play a part in the story you are telling? When scripture would reference going "up to Jerusalem" it didn't just mean going north. Depending on where they were, it could literally mean going up in elevation, particularly if they were in the Dead Sea area, which is the lowest elevation on earth. Explaining the distance between areas can also be enlightening since many people have not been to Israel before or are not familiar with the geography of the area. If you are talking about a country that no longer exists, you can include the present-day land.

> **If you have written a speech, you have a lot of the hard work already done when it comes to writing your book.**

Personal Stories

Make sure that you share personal stories that are relevant. We all like a good story but make sure that you get to the point. Don't feel the need to add unnecessary details. Leave names of others out if it will be hurtful.

Other's stories

You may want to share someone else's story. If you are using names, make sure to get their permission. It is sometimes best to tell the story without specifics. Just as with the personal story, it should be relevant and make sure that you get to the point. Leave names of others out if it will be hurtful.

Current Events

Is there something happening right now that can enhance your message or has something happened in the recent past that can enhance your story? If so, make sure that you use it. Don't forget to cite your sources. Do a Google search to see what is out there. You may be surprised.

Expert Opinions

It is always a good idea to see what the so-called experts are saying about your topic. This can result in great discussion and conversation. Give the reader a little background as to why you felt this was important. Make sure that you properly quote and cite your sources. Don't plagiarize! Give proper credit to the author and source.

Opposing View

Don't be afraid to state the opposing view to the position you are advocating for in your book. Defend your point strongly but politely. Make sure to cite your sources. Remember, we can agree to disagree. Be polite and don't fall into name-calling or belittling.

Understand That "Rough is Rough"

It is called a "rough draft" for a reason. It is rough, and that is fine. As you are writing your rough draft, resist the urge to stop and edit. This will hamper your creative flow. Just let the writing happen. You will have plenty of time to edit and rewrite later.

Moving Forward with the Manuscript

Once you have completed the rough draft, leave it alone for a few days before starting the editing process. As you start the editing process, remember your commitment to making this happen. Do not decide to trash it just because it doesn't sound right. If it doesn't sound right, fix it. Once you have spruced the rough draft up some, it is time to seek the help of a professional editor. They will help you transform your rough manuscript into a masterpiece.

Chapter 4 – Publish Your Book FAST

*W*oohoo! Congratulations. You have completed the rough draft for your book! This is no small feat. Make sure that you take time to celebrate your victory. You still have a little way to go before you cross the finish line and have your book in your hand, but you have come a long way.

Before we get into the nuts and bolts of publishing, we need to do a mindset check. This is where many aspiring writers get stuck. There are tons of unedited manuscripts sitting around on hard drives all over the world. Unfortunately, many of them stay unedited manuscripts and never become published books. You must decide right now, in this moment, that you will not allow that to happen to your manuscript. Promise me, and your manuscript, that you are going to see this through to the end. Don't let all this hard work go to waste. Let's do this. Alright, we can continue now...back to our regularly scheduled program. ☺ Let's talk about the editing and publishing process.

The Editing Process

We strongly suggest that you have your manuscript edited. Most experts agree that writers cannot edit their manuscripts. Of course, you have read and re-read your manuscript a number of times now and have probably found corrections each time. It is now time to turn it over to a fresh set of eyes. Let's look at the different types of editing available.

Basic Copyediting

Basic copyediting usually involves the editor reviewing your manuscript and providing corrections for typos, grammar, punctuation and spelling. This type of editing typically cost somewhere between $0.02 - $0.04 per word. For instance, a 10,000-word manuscript would cost somewhere between $200 - $400 for basic copyediting.

Comprehensive Copyediting

In comprehensive copyediting, the editor not only looks for typos, grammar, punctuation and spelling errors but will also provide recommendations on structure, plot, character development, and overall tone. This type of editing cost somewhere between $0.05 - $0.07 per word. A 10,000-word manuscript would cost somewhere between $500 - $700 for comprehensive copyediting.

Developmental or Substantive Editing

This type of editing will include all the elements of basic and comprehensive copyediting. In addition to that, it will include recommendations on the organization of the manuscript, sentence structure and rewriting text for flow and clarity. This type of editing will cost between $0.08 - $0.10 per word. A 10,000-word manuscript would cost somewhere between $800 - $1000 for this type of editing.

As the publisher, you can decide what type of editing is want for your manuscript. Remember, your work is a reflection on you and your company. You do not want to produce a book that is hard to read and full of mistakes. You want to put your best foot forward.

How to Find an Editor

You want to make sure that you choose the right person to edit your manuscript. There are many places online that offer editing services that are just a search away. You may also know someone who is qualified to edit your book. I use the word "qualified" for a reason. Everyone who reads your manuscript and points out a few errors is not necessarily qualified to edit your work. For instance, you need someone that is very familiar with grammar and punctuation rules. Many publishers use the "Chicago Manual of Style" as the standard for manuscript editing. If you choose not to hire a professional editor, try to find a retired teacher or perhaps a student that is majoring in English at a local college or university. There are many creative ways to get your manuscript edited so that you present your best work to the world.

Deciding Your Book Size

Before you can lay your book out, you must decide the size of your book. Most book printers offer a variety of sizes. Most of the paperback books we publish are 5" x 8" to 6" x 9". However, we have published color, pictorial books that were 8.5" x 8.5", 8" x 10" and 8.5" x 11". Book printers refer to this as the "trim size." There are several things you should consider when choosing a trim size. For a given manuscript, the smaller the trim size, the thicker the book. Do you have a number of pages you are aiming for? You may be able to tweak the font or margins to achieve the number of pages you desire. Also, think about how your reader is going to use the book. Does it need to fit in a purse or a pocket? Does it need to have enough room to write notes or journal entries?

> # There are tons of unedited manuscripts sitting around on hard drives all over the world.

Since many online retailers require "industry standard" trim sizes only, you need to consider how you plan to distribute your book especially if you are using non-standard sizes. You can use non-standard sizes, but it may mean that you will not be able to offer the book through popular online retailers such as Amazon or Barnes and Noble.

What do you do if you don't know what trim size is best? The best advice I can give; pick one. Choose a trim size, work with it and see how it fits your needs. You can always change it. Many times, you won't really know which size will work best until you begin the process of laying out your manuscript.

Cover Design

Once you have sent your manuscript off to editing and you have decided a trim size, it is time to work on the cover. Going back to our analogy of the book being your baby, the book cover is the outfit that you will present your baby to the world in. It must be perfect, right?

I wish I could tell you that people don't judge books by their covers, but they do. You want to make sure that your cover represents your book in the best possible light. Make sure that the colors are suitable and that the pictures are not stretched out. The last thing you want people to think is that you just threw something together.

You can have your cover professionally designed, but you must shop around for great quality at a great price. The graphic artists that I work with charge anywhere from $75 to $150 per cover. You can also get some great covers on <u>Fiverr.com</u>[iii] for a lot less.

I suggest that you have a couple of cover designs done and then ask your audience which cover they like the best. This is also a great way to start marketing your book. We will talk more about that in upcoming chapters.

While the cover is critical, don't make this an area of stress for yourself. Just like everyone is not going to like the outfit you have on, everyone is not going to like the cover you finally decide on. After you get everyone's feedback, it is ultimately up to you.

When I published my first book, I designed my book cover. It was the first book, and quite frankly, I didn't have an extra 100 bucks to drop on someone to do the cover, so I did it myself. It turned out "decent" in my opinion, not horrible (I have seen a lot worse) but not spectacular either. It was simply decent.

Several years after publishing the book, I met some new friends who hated my book cover. They were nice about it, but I knew that they weren't crazy about it. I thought about redesigning it, and I might still do that for the book's 10th year anniversary. But that cover grew on me. That cover represents more than just a book cover. It was the book cover for my first book, which launched my ministry and my business. Yes, it has sentimental value. I may decide to keep it a little longer.

But here is the crazy part. I was at a book vendor's event, and someone walked up to the table, grabbed the book and started reading the description on the back. They total me that the cover is what attracted them to the table and they when on to purchase the book. The moral of the story: you decide which cover best resonates with you and your message.

Speaking of book descriptions, make sure that you write a compelling description for the back of your book. People want to be able to pick your book up, read the description on the back and decide if they want to purchase it or not. The book description is not so much about the book as it is about the impact the reader can expect after reading it. I remember hearing long ago that people are tuned into WII-FM (What's in It for Me). You have 3-5 sentences to convince someone that your book is worth their time and money. Use those sentences wisely.

Book Layout

When laying out a book, you want to make sure that the book is appealing and easy to read. You also want to make sure that you have the headers and footers set properly. Nothing screams "homemade book" louder than ugly or missing headers, footers, page number and table of contents.

Printing Your Book

Now it is time to upload for printing. There are several print-on-demand companies with Amazon's KDP and Ingram Sparks being the major players at the time of this book's printing (May 2019). The process is pretty much the same with each company. You can open an account for free. You will add the information about your book including the title, author(s) and description and upload the manuscript and cover in separate files.

Once the book has gone through an initial quality check, you will be able to order your proof copy. If this is your first book, I strongly recommend that you order a proof copy. There is no feeling that compares to holding your first proof copy in your hand. Don't be surprised if you shed a tear. Out of the 100 plus authors I have published or coached, I don't know of any that did not cry when they received their proof copy in the mail. Although you are able to digitally proof the book, it doesn't take the place of seeing the actual book in your hands. It can be difficult to judge appropriate spacing and font size on the computer.

After you get over the excitement of having your proof copy in hand (trust me, you will be excited), it is time to read it. Read the proof copy. You will probably catch a few typos that you didn't catch before. If you find errors, correct the manuscript and upload again. If you only have minor typos, you don't need to order another proof. If you made major adjustments, you might want to order another copy to make sure that your changes resulted in the desired effect.

Once you have corrected all the errors, you are ready to approve your book. This is a BIG moment. When you press that "Approve" button, your book, your baby, is born. Get ready to shed a few more tears. All that hard work has paid off.

Post Publishing Errors

It happens to the best of us. You find an error in the book after you have approved it. Don't panic. While you can't do anything about the books that have sold already, you can upload the corrected manuscript so that the books going forward with be correct.

Chapter 5 – Promote Your Book FAST

Congratulations are in order here. You have not only written your book. You have published your book as well. We need to celebrate! Your book baby has been born. Let's bring out the champagne and cigars.

Well, I hate to be a party pooper, but I must interrupt this little shindig to ask an important question. Brace yourself.

You wrote a book. Now what?

I know, it may seem a little harsh, but someone must get your attention. I also know that I am adding more to your plate. Many authors write great books that sit out there in the virtual Amazon bookstore or gather dust in a garage. As an author, you may just write a book. But as a Chief Executive Author, you understand your mission is not just to write a book. You must maximize the value of that book.

We have talked about how to write and publish your book. Now it's time to promote your book. Well, let me correct that. The time to start promoting your book has passed. Ideally, you want to start promoting your book before you begin writing it. That way, you have an idea if people are even interested in the topic. Also, it allows you to start the marketing process. On average, it can take up to 6 to 8 "touches" or exposures to your offer to generate a sale.[iv]

Planning Your Book Signing

Although you may think of your book signing as a time of celebration and partying, it is also a time to start your book sales off with a bang. Your book signing will probably be one of the largest events that you have for selling your books. If this is your first book, many people will buy your book simply because it is you and you have written your first book. They want to celebrate and support you. That is a good thing!

Let's discuss a few ideas that will help make your book signing a success.

When to Schedule

When should you schedule your book signing? Once you have completed the second draft of your manuscript and you have decided that you are going to finish your project, it is probably a good time to start looking at dates for your book signing. At this point in the project, you are probably about 4-6

> Ideally, you want to start promoting your book before you begin writing it.

weeks away from completion so scheduling your book signing for any time after that is fine. When choosing your date, make sure to consider the schedule of your family, friends and target audience. For instance, a book signing on the Saturday before Easter or on a weekend where you know many of your friends will be out of town is probably not a great idea.

Where to Have It

This depends on the setting that you want, and the number of people you believe will attend. If you want a quiet, quaint setting, you may choose just to have a few friends over at someone's house. If you are expecting a larger audience, look into renting a meeting space. You can check your local church, YMCA or another hall rental facility.

Who to Invite

My opinion on this is simple, invite everyone, even those that you think may not be able to attend. Many people will still purchase your book, even if they are not able to attend your event in person. I advise my authors to make a list of at least 100 people. Start letting these people know early that you are writing a book and that you would appreciate their support.

What You Need for the Event

The first thing you need is your books. Make sure to order enough books so that everyone can purchase one. You don't want to run out of books at your book signing. You may also decide to have other promotional materials such as bookmarks, business cards or other cards that promote your book. Make sure to ask those that attend to spread the word about your project. This can result in additional book sales after your event.

Depending on your setting, you may decide to serve refreshments. How you do this will depend on your goals. I suggest that you do not spend a lot of money on hall rental and refreshments particularly if your goal is to make some money from your efforts. Hors-d'oeuvres, cake and punch may be enough. Having a cake that features the cover of the book is always a nice touch.

Book signings are exciting. Have fun celebrating your work and accomplishments.

Getting Paid

Make sure that you have at least one of these in place. I recommend that you have both. You can never be too prepared to accept payment.

PayPal[v]

It is hard to sell anything online without a PayPal account. PayPal allows you to accept all forms of payments anywhere you do business. Many online customers prefer PayPal because their financial data, such as credit card numbers, is not shared with the merchant. If you want to sell your book from your website or social media platform, you need to set up a PayPal account. It is fast and easy.

I suggest that you set up a separate bank account to link to your PayPal account. While PayPal accounts are relatively safe, they are not hack proof. You can generally open a new bank account with a $100 deposit.

There are two ways to get your money from PayPal once someone has paid you. You can transfer the money to your bank account, which usually takes a few days, or you can withdraw your cash using your PayPal debit card. Make sure that you order your PayPal debit card as soon as your account allows you to.

The PayPal Here app for your smartphone will allow you to accept credit cards and checks. This is a necessity if you are doing book signings and live events.

There are a few things you should keep in mind to keep your money safe with PayPal. Never give anyone the password to PayPal account. PayPal will never ask you for that information. Also, be careful of phishing emails that you may receive that appear to be from PayPal. Never click a link within an email that appears to be from PayPal. If the email indicates a problem with your account, close the email and log on to your account from PayPal's homepage. If you believe that your account has been compromised, contact PayPal as soon as possible.

Square UP[vi]

The Square is also a device that allows you to accept credit cards using your smartphone. This is a good alternative for on-site credit card acceptance if you don't have a PayPal account. You can also use it as a backup device in case you find that you need more than one processor. For instance, if you are at a large event and many people are in line to buy your book, you can have 2 "registers" going at once provided that you have access to a second smartphone. Transactions from Square are transferred to your bank account the next day. You can also track checks and gift certificates, but no funds are actually transferred.

Becoming an Amazon Bestseller

So many new authors don't understand what becoming an Amazon Bestselling Author does for their book and their brand. So, let me tell you...absolutely nothing. I'll explain.

Having the designation of being an Amazon Bestselling Author means that at some point in time, your books sold more copies in a particular category than other books. Since Amazon does its sales calculations on an hourly basis, this means that for a given hour, be it 1 PM or 3 AM; your book sold more. If five people bought your book around the same time of day, a few hours later, if you happened to check, you might see that your Amazon ranking has increased. It could even be #1 for that particular book category. That means that for a measly $5 (if your book was $0.99), you were a bestselling author. Yippee!

When you see that someone is an Amazon Best Selling Author, please understand that it doesn't mean that they have sold a ton of books and made a lot of money. It just means that for a moment in time, they sold more than others in their category.

So, should you try to be an Amazon Best-seller? Of course, you should. It's a cool designation, and it means something since most people don't understand how the system works. Therefore, when you post that your book is an Amazon Best-seller, people will stop, applaud, and congratulate you. That's great publicity. However, I don't want you falling into the trap of paying someone hundreds or thousands of dollars trying to figure out how to do it. It's pretty simple.

Host a virtual book launch. You can do a big, formal launch or do it livestream using a platform like Facebook Live. Use your Kindle book and set the price at $0.99. Get a couple of your super-friends to help and ask them to gift ten people books. This is great publicity for them as well. Do it late afternoon or evening. We have gotten people's books to #1 with as few as 30 sales.

Make sure that you watch your Amazon sales page to keep up with your ranking. Amazon does not store this information, so you must screenshot it yourself. Since it takes a few hours for Amazon's figures to update, start checking 3-4 hours after your event. Amazon does not designate books as best sellers. Authors typically do when their books hit certain rankings. Most of the time authors will wait until they are in the top 10 in their category, but some authors will call it at 100 or even 1000. Once you hit the designation you desire, make sure to post the screenshots on social media. It is great publicity and keeps the conversation going about your book. Hey, you will be $30 richer in a couple of months. Well, not really.

Once Amazon takes their cut, you'll end up with about $20. Don't spend it all in one place, big spender ☺.

Chapter 6 – Ways to Monetize Your Message

*N*ow that you have written and published your book, as a CEA, you have three goals. First, you must get your book into the hands of your reader. Second, you must explore ways to help your readers who want to implement your message do so. Finally, you must do so in a way that is financially beneficial to your bottom line. Let's me say it like this, you need to impact lives and make money doing so. It's just that simple.

Well, simple may be a slight exaggeration. It isn't complicated, but it does require work, planning and great foresight. There are some ways to provide more impact and monetize your message at the same time, and many of these ways don't require the creation of new content. Some of it is just packaging the content you have (your book) differently.

Here are 11 other products you can develop from your book.

- eBooks
- Audio Books
- Webinars
- Online Courses
- Teleseminars
- Speaking

- Certification Programs
- Membership Programs
- Special Reports
- Coaching
- Mobile Apps

Let's look at each of these.

eBooks

While eBooks sales have plateaued over the past few years, they are still an important part of your product line. Many readers prefer electronic versions to print. However, there are also many readers who like to have both. It is easy to access electronic books especially if you like to read while traveling. eBooks also make it easy to search for information. Since you don't have to create any new content to publish an eBook, it just makes sense to do it.

Kindle is probably the most popular platform for eBooks but don't forget about Nook and iBooks.

Tips When Writing Your eBook
Formatting Your eBook
The Kindle website allows potential buyers to preview the first 10% of your book. How does it look? Is it formatted properly? This could be a huge problem if you allowed your book printing company to format your book for Kindle automatically. You cannot just take the manuscript you used to print your book and publish it to Kindle. Well, you can, but it will look horrible. Not only do you have to take out the headers and footers, but you must make sure that you don't have extra spaces or not enough spaces so that it flows properly.

It is not hard to format a book so that it looks good on Kindle, but it does take work, and you need to know what you are doing. Amazon has even published a free Kindle book (<u>Building Your Book for Kindle</u>[vii]) designed to give you step by step instructions on how to format your book.

Take Advantage of Kindle Select Free Promo days

If you are a new author and you have not really established a following, you may be interested in participating in Amazon's Kindle Select program. It's a program for those that are willing to allow Kindle to be the exclusive distributor for their particular eBook for 90 days. If you agree, you can give your book away for free for up to 5 days in that 90-day period. I know you may be wondering why in the world would you want to GIVE your book away.

> You must understand that an eBook is not just an electronic version of your print book.

I thought this was about increasing sales. It is. If you do your book promo right, you will give 1000's of copies of your book away. Each of these free downloads will help your ranking and help get your name out there as an author and can even help you get some great reviews. The ranking you have during your free days, and the reviews that you get, if they are good, will increase your eBook sales when it comes off promo.

I didn't believe it either until I tried it, not once, not twice, but three times. I ran free promos for three different books, none of which had any Kindle sales before, and at least one of these books had been available on Kindle for almost two years with no sales. I found out how to get the word out about my promo and gave away almost 5000 books in the US and UK. In the three months after the promo, that eBook sold over 100 copies. Now, you may not think that's much, but that book had not sold anything before the promo. It also increased the sales of my other two books on the market.

Use Your eBook for List Building

You must understand that an eBook is NOT just an electronic version of your print book. It is an electronic version of your book that provides a gateway to instant access to everything else about your business, your brand and you. The links in your eBook are truly alive. I can click a link in your book and instantly go to that site without losing my place in your book. That is huge. You can direct traffic anywhere you want it to go.

My first book, Intensive Faith Therapy, was an inspirational book based on Bible lessons that could be used as an individual Bible study or part of a group study. When I first converted this to Kindle, I learned the hard way that you cannot just push a button and have a beautiful conversion without some major modifications. I developed an 80-page workbook out of the parts of the book that I could not use on Kindle such as the journal sections. When they clicked the link in my Kindle book, which was at the end of each chapter, they were taken to my website where they were asked for their email address. You know the drill from there; they sign up, confirm their email and were sent a link to download the workbook from my website.

Audiobooks

In addition to having your book available in digital format, you should also have it available as an audiobook as well. Many people prefer listening to audiobooks because they can listen while doing other tasks. Recording your audiobook is not hard at all and chances are you have everything you need on your smartphone or computer to produce a high-quality product. I have found that recording the audiobook before I approve the final print copy helps me to identify those last few typos that the editor, proofreader and I have missed.

Tips When Recording

Make sure that you are in a well-lit, comfortable area. You should have water available to hydrate during breaks. Relax and read as if you are having a one-on-one conversation with the listener. If you are reading fiction, consider changing your voice for different characters. You may even decide to have someone else read other parts for you. Keep a pen handy. Chances are, you will find a few mistakes that you didn't find before.

Don't try to do the entire book in one sitting. Take frequent breaks, especially after each chapter. Make it interesting. Don't sound as if you are reading a book. Draw the reader in with different voice inflections. Make sure that you use a good headset with mic to eliminate background noise.

Tools You Need

Audacity[viii] is an excellent, free program that can be used to edit audio recordings. As far as equipment goes, many people swear by the Blue Yeti Mic. It connects to your computer via USB. They cost around $100, and you can find them on Amazon.

Where to Publish

ACX,[ix] which is the audiobook arm of Amazon, is a great place to publish your audiobook. They allow you to market your book on Audible, Amazon and iTunes. You can also sell your audiobook directly from your site or another third-party platform.

Easy Digital Downloads[x] is a WordPress Plugin that allows you to sell your audio content from your site.

Sellfy[xi] will enable you to sell your audio content from their website for a small fee.

Webinars

Turning your book or other content into a webinar is an excellent way to repurpose and expand your content in terms of size, value and the amount you charge. Webinars also allow your audience to interact with you. This can lead to them to sign up for your higher priced programs.

You can do a webinar on your entire book or a particular chapter. The webinar can be free, or you can charge, depending on your strategy. Yes, you must have a strategy to use webinars effectively. For instance, you could do a free webinar covering an overview of your book as a list building activity. People would "pay" using their email address. You could also do paid webinars on specific chapters of your book. I have seen people charge anywhere from $25 to $97 for a single webinar.

Equipment and Software

You can use your laptop's video camera and sound system to start with, but you will probably want to invest in a better camera over time. I love my Logitech 920C camera, and the built-in microphone that comes with it is excellent.

There are several platforms out there, each with varying amounts of bells and whistles. I use Zoom.us which allows you to do webinars with invited guests. Other popular third-party sites include Webinar Jam and Goto Webinar.

Once you have recorded your webinar, your video will need somewhere to live. You may want to invest in a video storage platform such as <u>Amazon S3</u>[xii], <u>Wistia.com</u>[xiii] or <u>iPlayerHD.com</u>[xiv]. I don't recommend that you put your paid content on YouTube. YouTube is great for free content that you want to have available but remember, as a free platform, you have little control over how your content is displayed. Also, you don't want YouTube showing competitors ads on your videos.

If you want to edit your video before making it public, you will need video editing software. I love

Camtasia[xv]. It may seem a little pricey, but it's worth it. They normally run a free 30-day trial.

Other Things You Need

There are several other things you will need for your webinar. You will need to have some type of registration or landing page that people can use to sign up for your webinar. You will need to connect that opt-in form to an email management system, such as GetResponse. If you are charging for your webinar, you will need a payment gateway such as PayPal or Stripe.

Online Courses

One of the best ways to maximize the revenue from your book (remember your CEA mandate to maximize the value of your offerings) is to teach an online course based on your book. Not only does this produce additional revenue but it will allow your audience to take a deeper dive into your content and really apply your message to their lives. If you have a 10-chapter book, it would probably be easy to teach a class each week based on a chapter in the book.

How to Structure Your Course

Most online courses last for several weeks up to several months. I typically like to do courses that are 4, 6 or 10 weeks. Plan out your course based on how much information you can cover in about 30-45 minutes. This will allow you to have 15-30 minutes for discussion. If your book is long, don't try to teach everything that is in your book.

Courses usually consist of a weekly video/audio conference, pdf handout, and private Facebook group. All classes are recorded, and replays sent to registered participants or posted in the group. You can run your online class from your website, phone or one of the many teaching platforms out there.

How to Monetize

When planning your sales funnel, start with your online classes and then work out from there (lower priced items and higher priced items). You can charge for the entire class in one payment or allow weekly payments. Many people add an extra charge for those that are using a payment plan. That is usually in the form of a registration fee or an extra payment upfront to "save your seat." Consider offering discounts and other bonuses if the class is paid up front in full. You should consider offering a course for just about anything you have been asked about more than three times.

Tools/Technology You Need

Zoom.us[xvi] is an excellent platform for online classes. It is very affordable (at the time of this printing, Zoom is only $14.99 per month). You can have up to 100 people in your virtual classroom. After the class, you can download your videos to a service like iPlayerhd.com or Wistia.com and post the links to the replays in your Facebook group or email it to the list of participants. You will also need a landing page, an email management system and a payment system. If you want to offer quizzes or certificates, consider sites like Moodle[xvii] - or Udemy[xviii].

Teleseminars

Although we are in the video era, people still connect via telephone. Teleseminars provide a great platform for teaching a class or presenting content. As the name implies, it typically involves using a telephone conference platform to host your event. Many systems now include the capability to have people join from their computers as well. With teleseminars, you don't have to worry about the added pressure of being "video ready." You can do it in your pajamas. One of the added benefits of doing teleseminars is that the resulting audio can be sold after the live event is over. Your book is an excellent source of content, AND it can be used to increase book sales

How to Monetize

There are many strategic ways you can use teleseminars in the sales strategy for your book. You can host a weekly book club discussion or do a multi-week book review. You can do them for free (but require registration for list building) or for a fee. Many free teleseminars offer the replays as an upsell.

Tools/Technology You Need

There several excellent, free services available such as Free Conference Calling[xix] or Free Conference Call HD[xx]. There are also paid services as well such as UberConference[xxi]. This one isn't really made for teleseminars, but I love the feature that it will dial out to your participants at the correct time (if you set it up that way). Make sure you get a service that includes recording calls since you can download calls and use as a separate audio product.

You can store the audio downloads on services such as <u>SoundCloud</u>[xxii] or Audioboom[xxiii]. Use a program like Audacity to edit the audio if you choose to. It is one of the BEST free programs available. As always, you will need a landing page for registration and a way to accept payments, if offering a paid program.

Speaking

Growing your speaking business can be key to building other streams of revenue from your book. Speaking in public allows others to hear your message and the solutions to the problems you solve. While many people fear public speaking, the truth is, we do this every day in our businesses. Each sales call, support call or customer training we do is the basis of what we present to the public. As an author, it is important that you strategically use speaking to grow awareness of you, your book and your brand.

Where to Speak

While it may not seem like it at first, there are tons of places where you can speak. You can do retreats, seminars or other types of live events. Schools are always looking for someone to give speeches and motivational talks to the children and staff and colleges, in particular, often have a budget for speakers. Furthermore, don't sit back and wait for someone else to ask you to speak on their stage. Create your own stage! Consider hosting your own live event and don't forget about online livestreaming platforms like Periscope, Facebook Live, YouTube Live and Instagram Live.

Getting Paid

Establish a speaking fee. You may decide to waive it for a particular organization but do not become branded as a "free speaker." (If you waive the fee, send a paid invoice and ask for a letter for your taxes). If you are being asked to waive your fee, ask if you can sell product from the stage or back of the room. Many speakers make more from the back of room sales than they do from the honorarium. Don't forget to ask for a testimonial after your speech. You can use that on your website to attract more speaking engagements.

> Growing your speaking business can be key to building other streams of revenue from your book.

Find out if the host is planning on selling the recording of your speech. You need to either have rights to sell it as well or be compensated for your speech.

Preparation

Try to get an idea of who the audience is and make sure that they will find your message helpful. Do not just pitch your product or solution. Whatever you talk about, make sure to tie it in with one of your books. Consider prerecording your speech and have the audio available for sale as well. If you are nervous about speaking, consider joining a local Toastmasters[xxiv] Club.

Tools/Technology You Need

You will need a media kit and a speaker one sheet. The speaker one sheet reminds me of a graphic resume' that highlights your speaking accomplishments. Make sure that you have a way to accept payment on site (Square, PayPal Here or Stripe). Always offer a free lead magnet to get people to sign up on your list. Most organizers will not share with you the list of attendees. Consider having a postcard available that has the following links on it:

- Link to buy your book and other products/services

- Link to book you for other speaking engagements

- Link to schedule a discovery session with you

Certification Programs

Certification programs allow you to train others to do what you do. You allow them to share your expertise with their audience, for a fee. Think of it as "franchising" for your brand. This is probably one of the best ways to protect your intellectual property since people are naturally going to share what they learned. This way, they are free to share it as a "certified coach" from your brand.

How to Structure Your Program

You can take just about any book or course that you have and develop a "train the trainer" program. Most certification programs include some type of assessment such as quizzes, tests or graded projects. You can certify one class or a series of classes. You can also develop a network of "certified" people that are featured on your website and/or social media.

Many programs include a one-time fee and a yearly recertification fee. This is typically one of your higher priced programs since programs like this are usually priced over $1000. Make sure to have guidelines in place, including guidelines on how someone can lose their certification. Have an intake process where you screen candidates carefully. Remember, they will represent your book and brand.

Tools/Technology You Need

You can use much of the same technology used for online classes. You may want to integrate an LMS (Learning Management System) into your WordPress site or use a third-party platform. Learndash[xxv] allows you to integrate into a WordPress environment (Cost $160-$330). Of course, you will need a landing page, CRM (Email management) and payment system.

Membership Programs

Membership programs are an excellent way to build your community, deliver great content and build your bank account. In a membership program, your customers pay each month/quarter/year to access your content. If you deliver great content, membership programs can be a great stream of revenue and provide a great community of people that may be interested in your higher priced services.

For authors, this can be a great opportunity. Consider trying this. First, let me be transparent. I got this idea from one of my mentors, Trevor Otts. Consider starting your own book club. Charge a nominal fee, like $10 a month, and as a bonus, you can include a copy of the book. Each month host a discussion about one chapter in your book. You can do it via teleseminar or video using a private Facebook group. If you have a 12-chapter book, this can provide content for a year. Even if your book is only ten chapters, you can easily stretch it out to a year. By the end of the year, you should have completed your next book. 😊 Instead of getting $10-$15 per book, you will get $120 per book.

Membership programs are my favorite because the pricing model is so powerful.

You can build a membership portal on your site where your clients must have the password to access premium content, or you can use a private Facebook group to deliver content as well. You may also want to deliver content via email. The best programs use a combination.

Pricing Model

This is the magic of membership programs; there is recurring revenue so you don't have to sell the same person every month. However, you must continue to provide great content or people will quit. You want to continue marketing the program so that you can account for attrition. You may want to expand your membership program to not only cover the information in your book but also how to implement the principles. This would be a more expensive membership program.

Membership programs are my favorite because the pricing model is so powerful. Let's look at some numbers!

What if you wanted to make an extra $20,000 in the next 12 months from a $25 product?

$20,000/$25 = 800 units (or customers)

800 units/12 months = 67 units a month

You need to make 67 sales EACH month

Not very hard, comes out to about three sales a day. Three sales a day isn't very hard, but you will have to be very diligent making sure that you met your target every day. Let's look at an easier way. Here is how to make an extra $20,000 in 12 months from a $25 monthly membership

$20,000/12 months = $1,667 per month

$1,667 / $25 = 67 people

If you keep those 67 people happy, you don't have to find another 67 people next month. The membership automatically bills them. Even if you lose five people a month, you only must make 122 sales throughout the year to replace them instead of 800. You can spend more time concentrating on producing great content.

Tools/Technology You Need

You can build on your own site using WordPress and a membership plugin like wp-eMember[xxvi], MemberPress[xxvii], Paid Membership Pro[xxviii] or a number of other ones. There are third-party platforms like Wishlist[xxix], Memberclicks[xxx], or a ton of others available as well. You will need to connect to your payment system and email management system as well and don't forget your landing page, graphics, and payment system that supports recurring or subscription payments.

Special Reports

Special reports or lead magnets are a necessary component for any list building activity. While you don't typically sell these, these can be responsible for other sales in your business because they are offered in exchange for an email address. Special reports are writings that are much shorter than an eBook. They can range from 1-3 pages up to about 20 pages. You can produce a special report about any subtopic within your topic of interest. You can take portions of your book and produce these special reports.

If you are using this as a lead magnet, it should focus on answering one key question. They help establish you as an expert. The title must be compelling enough for someone to want to give you their email address in exchange for it. Avoid putting too much into a lead magnet. Typically, these documents are delivered in PDF format. Make sure to put "Copyright" on the page and include a link back to your website.

Tools/Technology You Need

You can produce these in Word® and save as a PDF or, if you really want to jazz it up, you can produce an Infographic on Canva[xxxi] or another platform. You will need a place to store your document where people can download it. Most email management systems like GetResponse[xxxii] have this feature. You will need a landing page where people can fill out an opt-in form to receive the download. You must have an autoresponder set up to deliver the report any time of day.

Coaching

Coaching is a billion-dollar industry and will continue to grow for the foreseeable future. There as so many types of coaches nowadays that it is hard to keep up with. Some coaches will help you with business, life, career, grief, writing, publishing and just about anything else that you need help with. Why is coaching so popular? Because people need someone to help them with issues such as accountability and getting over limiting beliefs. Unlike a consultant, a coach does not have to be an expert in the type of business that their clients are in. You bring a holistic approach to your client's situation. Often, being in a different industry can be beneficial because you can help your clients see things from a different perspective.

As an author, your book can provide the perfect foundation for your coaching program. You have already given them the information. Now it is time for you to show them how to implement and take action. This can truly be life-changing for your reader.

Types of Programs

Group Coaching

Group coaching is an excellent way to serve more people at one time. The dynamics of a group can be powerful. Your program can occur by phone, in person or even online, like in a private Facebook group or Zoom meeting. Prices typically range from $29 - $99 per person/ per session or a flat fee for a series of sessions.

Individual Coaching

Individual coaching is a more in-depth coaching program that requires more of your time and is, therefore, more expensive. Prices can range from $97 to over $1000 per session. You can offer a package or bundle, giving a discount if they purchase more than one session at a time.

VIP Days

VIP days are exclusive, high-end coaching events where people pay to spend the entire day with you, working on their business or issue. This can be in person or virtual. Since this requires much more involvement from you, these packages are more expensive. Prices can start around $2000 and go up to $20,000 depending on the type of program you offer.

Chief Executive Author

Tips to Get Started Coaching

Begin with having a general price per session. This will prevent you from having people pick your brain for free. This is key. You can offer a free 15-20-minute discovery session. The goal of this session is to get an understanding of what they need, not to try to solve all their problems in 20 minutes. I learned from one of my coaches, Larry Beacham, that you can tell people what they need and why they need it for free. When you start to tell them HOW to achieve it, you should be charging.

Tools/Technology You Need

You will need a scheduling program that will allow people to sign up for an appointment. Don't go back and forth with people on scheduling. Give them the link to your calendar and let them go from there. There are several great programs out there, such as <u>Timetrade</u>[xxxiii], <u>Acuity Scheduling</u>[xxxiv], <u>Calendy</u>[xxxv].

Of course, you will need a payment system, such as <u>PayPal</u>[xxxvi], <u>Stripe</u>[xxxvii], <u>Square</u>[xxxviii] or <u>Moonclerk</u>[xxxix]. Invest in a conference calling system like <u>UberConference</u>[xl]. Their paid program is only $10 per month. Free systems look tacky if you are charging. If you are doing video conferences, <u>Zoom.us</u>[xli] is great.

Mobile Apps

Can you imagine a thriving business existing today without a website? That is precisely how it will be in a few years when it comes to mobile apps. Not only will it be critical from a customer engagement standpoint, but it

72

will also be essential to your bottom line. The app industry hit over $60 billion in 2017 and is expected to double over the next four years.

Having an app for your book is a great way to get people involved in your message and to continue to have ongoing engagement with them. Your app can include many of the same components as your website. Make sure to include great content and make it easy for people to connect with you via social media. Don't forget to incorporate rewards. People love to be rewarded.

Your app can be free or paid, but most free apps make more money in the long run through paid advertisement. But you can also offer a premium version of your app that is ads free. Sign up for an ads account with Google or other third party such as StartApp[xlii]. Apps developers can make a couple of dollars a month to a couple of thousands a month.

Tools/Technology You Need

You can hire a contractor to develop your app using a service like Upwork.com[xliii] or learn to do it yourself on sites like AppyPie[xliv] or AppMakr[xlv]. Make sure to have your app available for iOS and Android.

Your Product Line

You can develop your product line by choosing several items from the list above. Every product line can have different components, and it is based on your market and how your target audience likes to receive content.

I believe that every product line should have a book. All publishing biases aside (well, most of them aside), I can't think of any business that would not benefit from having a book. A book is a great way to inform and educate your audience, and it is a great way to establish yourself as an expert. Of course, once you have the book, you have the content for the eBook and the audiobook. You kill three birds with one stone.

Webinars, teleseminars and special reports can be used to promote your other products such as classes, coaching, and membership programs. Online courses are great because they allow you to share your content with many people at one time. Membership programs are one of my favorite offerings because it is a source of recurring revenue. Speaking opportunities are always great because you can share your message live and generate interest for other products you have. Think about your message, the problems you solve, and the people you solve those problems for and then develop your product line.

Now that we understand the bottom line of business, and we have our products and services in place, the fun begins. Let's get these great solutions into the hands of our target market.

Chapter 7 – Sales Funnels

*M*arketing is the biggest tool you have as an author to get your book in the hands of your target audience. So, what exactly is marketing?

According to the American Marketing Association (yes, that's a real organization) marketing is:

> *The activity, set of institutions, and processes for creating, communicating, delivering, and exchanging offerings that have value for customers, clients, partners, and society at large.*[xlvi]

In laymen's terms, marketing is how you inform, educate and convince your reader that your book can meet their needs, which is the third element in our Bottom Line of Business. Before we dive into exactly HOW to do this, we must understand the basics of marketing relationships. Marketing relationships follow the same rules as human relationships because, at the end of the day, businesses don't buy from businesses. It is people in business who buy from other people in business. This is what I call the Relationship Based Marketing Methodology.

Overview of the Relationship Based Marketing Methodology

You need to use your digital marketing power to cultivate relationships with people. Just as in human relationships, you can move too fast in marketing/social media relationships. You would find it awkward and weird for someone to ask you to go away with them for a week's vacation to a foreign place on a first date. Even if you wanted a vacation and had told your friends about how you wanted to visit a certain destination, you would be leery about going away with someone you just met.

Why? It isn't the offer. You love vacations; you love to travel, you have always wanted to go to that destination. It's not the offer; it's where you are in relationship with the person that is making the offer. I can have the best products and services in the world,

> Marketing is the biggest tool you have as an author to get your book in the hands of your target audience.

and they could be the exact products and services you need, but if I don't take time to cultivate a relationship with you, you will not buy my book or my service.

One of my social media pet peeves is for someone to send me a message on Facebook Messenger asking me to buy their book, especially if I don't know them. I know, it's only a $10 book. It wouldn't matter if it were free. You still must convince me that it is worth my time to get your book. You must take the time to develop a relationship with me.

However, great relationships and good vibrations are not enough to build a truly successful business. You need to have a few digital marketing systems in place.

In the next two chapters, we will cover the first five systems that you need to master in your business as a Chief Executive Author. These are:

- Your Sales Funnel
- Your Marketing Content
- Your Paid Traffic
- Your Social Media Presence
- Your Email Marketing

Your Sales Funnel

What makes a good date? Is it the magnificent restaurant, the stimulating conversation or the surprise gift you received at the beginning of the evening? Is it any ONE thing or is it the experience as a whole?

In my opinion, the whole idea of "marketing" is taking your prospective client on a series of fantastic dates, with each date designed to strengthen the relationship. As with human relationships, the goal is not just to reach one moment in time, i.e., the altar. The goal is to "grow old together."

Your sales funnel is a set of sequences designed to do just that. The purpose is to move the relationship forward. It is about giving your clients one great experience with you after another. You may start out solving a small problem for your client with a low-cost product. The goal is to progress so that you are solving more complex problems for your client with higher priced solutions.

Typically, your sales funnel will have the following components:

- Ungated Information
- Lead Magnet
- Tripwire Offer
- Core Offer
- Upsell Offer
- Downsell Offer

Let's look at each of these.

Ungated Information

Consider the following scenario. Imagine you are at a function and you catch the eye of someone that is interested in meeting you. They come over to you, introduce themselves to you, and you begin chatting. You may talk about why you are at the function or something related to the function that you both have in common. After chatting it up for 30 minutes, you realize that this is a nice person and you wouldn't mind seeing them again.

At the end of the conversation, you exchange cards and make a promise to keep in touch or even meet for coffee in a few days.

That sounds like the beginning of a great relationship. Even if you remain friends, things have started on a good note. You are probably more likely to respond to their text messages or phone calls the next day because the evening didn't go like this...

Imagine you are at a function and you catch the eye of someone that is interested in meeting you. They come over to you, introduce

If you waste people's time, they will not give you their money.

themselves to you, and you begin chatting. Immediately they start to try to sell you on their product, service or themselves. They tell you that you are crazy if you talk to anyone else at the gathering because they have everything you will ever need. But you better act fast if you want to take advantage of this great opportunity. For you to demonstrate that you are worthy of this opportunity, you need to have some "skin in the game." They are convinced that if you let them, they can grow your business, expand your products or be the love of your life. But you must act now. So, they ask you to invest in yourself by purchasing their $997 product or going somewhere with them that is a little more "private."

Most likely, you will not have to ignore this person's texts or calls because you probably didn't give them your information anyway. You got far, far away from this person as soon as you could.

Why was scenario one better for relationship building? You were able to get to know the person first before you committed to moving to the next level. Although the "next level" only consisted of giving your contact information, that is a big next step for entrepreneurs.

As entrepreneurs, we hate unproductive contact. That includes unwanted emails, social media messages, and text messages. Admit it; you have screened your calls before. You have glanced at your Messenger before and decided NOT to click it because you didn't want the person to know you had seen their message. People must earn the right to get our attention.

That is exactly what ungated information does for you as a business owner. It helps you earn the right to get the attention of your audience. This is information that people can get that requires no commitment on their part. You are demonstrating your knowledge about the topic and how that knowledge can help them. This information should not require any information for them to access it. Although this information is free, it must be GOOD. If you waste people's time, they will not give you their money.

Examples of other ungated information include:

- Blog posts on your site
- Blog posts on LinkedIn
- Livestream
  - Periscope
  - Facebook Live

If your ungated information is useful, people will want to move forward in the relationship. However, you must have something for them to move forward to.

Lead Magnet

Now it's time to get some information. Remember scenario 1? If you enjoyed the conversation with that person, in order to have another conversation you will have to give up some information. If you are going to "keep in touch" you must provide contact information for that to happen.

In your marketing, this is done with what is known as a lead magnet, or freemium. This is free, quality content that solves one problem in exchange for an email address. In addition to developing content that can be used as a lead magnet (we will cover that in a later chapter), you must have a way to capture the email address and deliver the content.

This is where you begin the gift giving part of the relationship, but the gift cannot be random. The lead magnet should lead to your tripwire and core product. Also, make sure that the lead magnet is appropriate for where your customer is in their journey with you. When first meeting someone, inviting them to coffee to continue a great conversation is great. Inviting them to go away with you for the weekend to continue the conversation is a little creepy.

Tripwire

Now the fun begins. It is time to get a commitment. This is the point where you make an offer for your potential customer to become a real customer. It's time for them to pull out their credit card.

Your tripwire offer should be a low priced, high-value item. Depending on your market, it should be priced under $20 ($7 has tested to be the optimal price). It should have a valued of $49 to about $200.

There are many in the digital marketing community that swear by the use of tripwire offers. There are others that are dead set against them. What's the answer? You should try it for yourself and your market. I have seen a lot of success with them.

Your book is an excellent tripwire offer. Most books are priced under $20, and it gives the reader the opportunity to get to know you and your message in an intimate way. Examples of other tripwire offers include:

- Workshop or Class
- One module of a multi-module series
- Evergreen audio or video recordings

Tripwire offers are typically "do it yourself" solutions which have little to no direct access to you. The customer must read the book or watch the videos and then implement the solutions on their own.

Core Offer

Your core offer should drive your entire funnel. What you offer as a lead magnet and tripwire should lead to the purchase of your main product. Since you may have many products in your business, you may have many sales funnels.

What is your core offer? This is where many authors mess up. Many authors will tell you that their book is the core offer. It is not, especially for the Chief Executive Author. Your book is your business card. It is the teaser to your higher priced products and services. You must have something in place beyond the book.

Many authors tell me that they would love to develop an online class, coaching or membership program based on their book, but they just haven't gotten around to it yet. What?!!! You are leaving a ton of money on the table! That is like telling me that you have $10,000 scattered on your floor and you are so stressed trying to figure out how to pay your $1,000 mortgage that you don't have time to pick up the $10,000 that is on your floor because you are too stressed about your mortgage. Where is a good, "Are you crazy!" meme when you need it?

Some authors say that they are waiting for the book to take off first and THEN they will develop something bigger. I say develop something bigger FIRST so that the book can take off.

If you haven't done so already, go back to the chapter on product development and figure out what your core offer is going to be that is based on your book. Online courses, coaching programs, and membership programs make great core offers.

This is often a "do it yourself" or "done with you" solution. Also, this product offers limited access to you. The more of your time that is involved in delivering the solution, the higher the price.

> **You must have something in place beyond the book.**

Upsell

This is a more extensive version of your core product and is often the "done for you" solution to your core product. It may be add-ons that your core product doesn't offer.

We have seen upsells used in marketing often, but we may not have been aware of it. When you buy a new car, some features come standard (that's the core offer). If you want to get additional features, you must upgrade (that's the upsell).

As an author, your upsell could be your one-on-one coaching or your exclusive VIP days where the reader will spend time with your personally to figure out how to implement the strategies or principles outlined in your book.

Downsell

Sometimes your upsell package is more than your client needs. You can offer what is known as a downsell offer which is a lower priced option of your upsell package. This package doesn't offer as much as the upsell, but it is still higher priced than the core product. Please note, this is NOT your Upsell product ON sale.

Pulling it all together

Go through your product offerings and determine your tripwire, core offers, upsell and downsell offers. Now that you have your inventory of products and services organized, it's time to start marketing. Remember, we said earlier that marketing is just giving your client one great experience after another. Also, the third pillar of our "bottom line of business" is to inform, educate and convince our customers that we can meet their needs. Content Marketing is how we can bring all of this together.

Chapter 8 - Content Marketing

*W*hat is content marketing? Well, let's look at what content is. Content is anything an individual or brand creates for consumption.[xlvii] This includes blog posts, photographs, videos, audios, infographics, and social media posts. Content Marketing is when you use this created content to bring more awareness to your message, your brand and yourself. I include "yourself" because you must realize that everything you post on social media is content.

We see it happen every day to celebrities. Something they said 20 years ago when no one knew their name, comes back to haunt them. You may not see yourself as a celebrity, but you are. The world may not be judging your every move, but someone is. Someone is looking at what you post and deciding if they want to work with you or not. You may think that there is such a thing as a "personal" Facebook page but in reality, it isn't. If you are in business, which if you are an author you are, then anything you post, whether it is on your personal page or your business page, represents your brand.

Types of Content for Marketing

While there are tons of ways to use content marketing, let's focus on the three that I have found to be the most effective: livestream, video, and blogging.

Livestream

A livestream is a live broadcast transmission over the internet. Unlike video, which is pre-recorded, livestream is happening...well...live. Several social media platforms allow this with Periscope, Facebook Live and YouTube Live being a few of the most popular. Livestream allows you to engage with your audience in real time. You can use this to talk about your book, upcoming classes or just shoot the breeze.

I must admit, I learned just about everything I know about livestream from the Queen of Livestream, Dawniel Winningham. Although I was on Periscope the first day it was released, I didn't understand how to use it to monetize my message until I got into Dawniel's Livestream class – Scope School.

One of the most powerful things about livestream is that it helps you see the power that you have as a media company. Yes, you are a media company. With your livestream accounts, you can develop programs just like a television station. You can stream entertainment, educational or inspirational content at the push of a button. That content can reach your followers and the followers of your followers if they choose to share it.

With all that power comes responsibility. You must be consistent. You must prepare. You must have a strategy in place. If not, you will have all this power at your fingertips and either misuse it or worse, not use it all.

Livestream Strategies for Authors

There are a number of ways that you can use livestream in your marketing strategy as an author. These are just a few.

Before the Book is Complete

- Do a livestream to talk about your upcoming book and see what your audience thinks about the topic. Is this something that your audience is interested in? Does your book answer a question that your audience has?

- Behind the Scenes – Do livestreams while you are in the writing process. Let your audience know what you are thinking about as you are writing and get their feedback.

When the Book is Complete

- Do a livestream when you get your first order of books. Share the excitement of having completed the project. Let them know how excited you are that this information is now available that will help them with whatever problem your book solves.

- Book Readings – Do livestream book readings to share portions of your book and generate discussion on specific topics.

- Additional Products – Do livestreams to talk about the additional products and services that are coming as a result of your book.

Video

When it comes to marketing, it seems that video makes everything perform better. Social media posts with video get more engagement than those without. Landing pages with video have higher conversion rates than those that don't. Look at these amazing statistics from Wordstream[xlviii].

- 82% of Twitter users watch video content on Twitter

- YouTube has over a billion users, almost one-third of total internet users.

- 45% of people watch more than an hour of Facebook or YouTube videos a week.

- More than 500 million hours of videos are watched on YouTube each day.

Many authors get spooked when it comes to videos. I have heard countless authors complain about how they don't like the way they look on video and how they can't stand to hear themselves recorded. Well, let me share this valuable piece of advice with you – GET OVER IT. It's just that simple. Now I could tell you that you can do videos and not even be in the videos and that is true. I could tell you that you could have someone else do the videos for you and that is true, although not very effective. But the bottom line is that people want to connect with you, the author. We are our own worst critics. So, I ask you, as one of my coaches, Bob Doyle, asked me once, "How big do you want to play in this space?" If you want to build a successful brand from your book that will impact the lives of many people, you must get over yourself and do what needs to be done to accomplish the first element in the Bottom Line of Business. You must find your customers or make it easy for them to find you. Video content will achieve that.

Video Strategies for Authors

As an author, there are a number of ways that you can use video as part of your marketing strategy. For starters, you can take the recorded videos from each of the livestreams that you did in the previous section and post those videos on your social media pages and website to promote your book. You can also take each of those topics listed in the livestream section and pre-record them as videos and post them as well.

You should have a video trailer for your book. This is a short video, typically less than 2 minutes, that talks about your upcoming book. You should also have a welcome video on your website and even on your social media pages that lets people get to know you and your brand better. However, make sure that you are sharing valuable content in these videos. Content marketing is not about promoting your book. It is about sharing great content that connects to your book. Content marketing is designed to paint you as an expert, not a salesperson.

Blogging

One of the easiest and most effective marketing strategies you can use in your business is blogging. Blogging allows you to publish relevant content while increasing the exposure of you and your brand to your target market. Blogging, when done right, can help you build your list, engage with your audience and increase your sales. As an author, this can translate into more book sales and increased revenue from your other products and services.

If your website is built in WordPress, you already have a place to publish your blog articles. It's as simple as writing a "post" and hitting publish. If you don't have a website, you need to get one. While you can blog on free third-party sites, most of those sites do not allow you to use your blog for commercial purposes. Remember, we are not blogging for our health. These blogs are part of our marketing strategy. We are trying to make sales here!

Here are a few reasons why you need to take your business' blog seriously.

Blogging allows you to create content that will attract your target audience.
While we often credit Google for providing information about anything we can think of, the truth is, Google provides very little of the content that we find on the web. Google is just a search engine. What is it searching? It is searching all the content that has been published on the internet by people like you and me. When you search

"how to build a landing page," Google goes to its handy-dandy index and gives you a list of all the pages on the web that talk about 'building a landing page." Those pages, many of those blog posts, were written by people just like us, who have something to say about

> **Blogging, when done right, can help you build your list, engage with your audience and increase your sales.**

building landing pages. When you click on a particular post, you are taken AWAY from Google and TO the website that the content is found on. From there, you can read the article or click around to see if there is other information on the site that you are interested in.

Blogging allows your content to be searchable.
Let's say that you wrote a great Facebook post on how to build a landing page. Guess what? The person we mentioned above that is searching on Google for that topic will never find your post. Why? Content that you post on Facebook is NOT searchable on Google. Most content that is posted on social media is NOT searchable through search engines. For your content to be searchable, it must be on your website or a third-party platform such as YouTube which is searchable by Google (especially since Google owns YouTube).

Blogging allows you to showcase your expertise.
Your blog content allows you to showcase your knowledge and expertise. Readers will have a chance to experience how you can help them solve their problem. When you can produce several targeted pieces of content in a given area, it increases your credibility.

However, blogging is not just about writing a bunch of content and posting it on your website. Blogging is a main source of ungated content and therefore an essential part of your sales sequence. Blogs are sometimes the first introduction that someone has to you or your products and services.

Content Marketing is a great way to inform, educate and convince your customers that you can meet their needs. However, having great content is not enough. You must drive traffic to that content and get people to see it.

Chapter 9 – Paid Traffic

*H*aving books, products, and services, along with well thought out content to promote them, is great but you must make sure that someone sees all this great stuff you offer. People cannot respond to your offer if they don't see it.

Unfortunately, just because there are millions of people surfing the internet and hanging out on social media, it doesn't mean that they are looking at your website or engaging with your social media posts. You must drive traffic to your content.

Traffic comes in two forms, paid and unpaid. In a perfect world, you would put a post on social media or release an article on your blog announcing your book and people who have the problem that your book solves would flock to Amazon or your site to buy your book. Well, it just doesn't happen that way. The line, "Build it, and they will come," was great in the movie "Field of Dreams" but not in real life. You must go get your traffic, at least to begin with.

Unpaid traffic, also known as "organic" traffic, happens when someone comes to your website without you paying for it. Maybe they searched something on

Google, and your page came up in the search results, and they clicked the link to arrive at your site. They may follow you on social media and saw a post or someone might have told them about your book. They may have even searched for something on Google, and your Amazon book listing came up.

Organic traffic is great; however, it is not always plentiful. You must do a lot of work to get your website to the point where it will receive a lot of traffic organically. While there are some Search Engine Optimization (SEO) things you can do, the complicated algorithms that Google and other search engines use make it virtually impossible to count on organic traffic to get in front of the right people. This makes it difficult when you are first starting. That is why you must include a paid traffic strategy in your digital marketing plan.

Paid Ads

I believe that paid ads are the best way to get targeted traffic to your offers, especially when you are first starting. However, you must have a strategy that accounts for the relationship-based business methodology that we discussed in the introduction. This is where I believe many authors and entrepreneurs make their mistake when it comes to using paid ads. You still must make sure that you are making the correct offer to the right people based on where you are in relationship with them.

You can purchase ads on just about every social media platform out there. Each platform has its own requirements, and there are so many strategies out there, it would require a book by itself. So, instead of trying to explain each of the platforms, I include a resource list from each specific platform that you can use to find out more information.

- Facebook[xlix]
- Instagram[l]
- LinkedIn[li]
- Twitter[lii]
- Google[liii]
- YouTube[liv]
- Pinterest[lv]
- Snapchat[lvi]
- Bing[lvii]
- Yahoo[lviii]

Targeting the Right Audience

Figuring out the right audience for a given ad can be one of the most complicated parts of the ad process. That is why it is so important that you figure out your customer/reader avatar. An avatar is a fictional character that represents your ideal prospect.[lix] It's not important to just know what problems your target market has and what keeps them up at night. You need to know where these people hang out, especially in cyberspace. What sites do they visit? What social media platforms are they on and who are they following on those platforms? If you get this wrong, and you will from time to time, you will find that your ads are not effective.

So, what do you do? You make your best guess, based on your customer avatar, and tweak it as necessary. See what works and look at what doesn't work. Do your research and don't be afraid to try.

Retargeting

It's happened to you before. You went on a site, like Amazon or Best Buy, and looked at something, maybe a new laptop. You spent a few moments on the site and then decided to do something else. Later that day, you were on Facebook, and to your surprise, an ad shows up on Facebook for the EXACT item you were looking at before on Amazon. The next day, you go to Yahoo and BAM, there it is again. You notice for the next several days these ads appear to follow you on social media.

> You must drive traffic to your content.

Welcome to the world of retargeting. Retargeting is a technology-based method that allows your offer to follow people who have been on your site. It is extremely effective because people need to see your offer more than once. Studies have shown that only 2% of web traffic will convert on the first visit. Retargeting allows you to digitally "follow up" with people who have been on your site.

Retargeting uses a simple JavaScript code. You place a pixel, a small piece of code, on your website. It's that simple. The pixel can't be seen and will not affect your site's performance. When someone new visits your site, the code drops a cookie in their browser. When you run ads targeting those that have this cookie, your ad will be shown to those people. This is a powerful tool that can increase your conversion rates tenfold.

However, Facebook recently announced that they are instituting new privacy measures which will allow people to opt out of being tracked with the Facebook pixel. If someone opts out, the pixel will not track their data so you will not be able to retarget them.

Where Should You Be

One of the questions most asked is, "What social media platforms should I advertise on?" The answer is simple, the ones where your target market is. However, with that said, I think you should venture out a little into other platforms sometimes. Why? Because you never know exactly where people hang out. So, don't be afraid to spend a few dollars trying out new platforms. Don't spend your entire ad budget there but you may want to shake things up from time to time.

Chapter 10 - Social Media

"We don't have a choice on whether we do social media, the question is how well we do it."

Erik Qualman

*R*egardless of what you think about social media, you must get in the game to get more readers and grow your business. While having a website is extremely important, people are not typically hanging out on your website. People will come to your site to get what they need and then they will leave. Since most websites are not designed in such a way as to encourage dialogue or interaction, you need to go where the people are. People are hanging out on social media. They are posting their information on Facebook, their pictures on Instagram, their random thoughts on Twitter and their questions in LinkedIn groups. We will discuss more details about your social media strategy in a later chapter.

At the time of this writing (July 2019), these are some of the top social media platforms[ix]. Do you have a presence on these?

- Facebook - 2.3 Billion Estimated Unique Monthly Visitors

- YouTube - 2.0 Billion Estimated Unique Monthly Visitors

- Instagram - 1 Million Estimated Unique Monthly Visitors

- Twitter - 330 Million Estimated Unique Monthly Visitors

- LinkedIn - 310 Million Estimated Unique Monthly Visitors

- Pinterest - 265 Million Estimated Unique Monthly Visitors

These social media sites are phenomenal tools for finding customers and being found by customers. With over a billion unique monthly visitors, they have become a hub for all things social. This means that they have become a hub for all things business because many people conduct business is a "social way." This is nothing new. Back in the day, many deals were brokered on golf courses and in country clubs. Today it is Facebook fan pages, Messenger and LinkedIn connections that people are using to expand their sales and networks.

Make sure that your social media presence represents the best side of you. Although it may be tempting to air your dirty laundry and lash out about people and issues, consider how this will look to your customers. Remember, what you share on Facebook and any other social media can be shared or captured (via screenshot) and disseminated to the world.

Housekeeping

While you may not be active on all social media platforms, I believe that you should have a presence on all of them. At a minimum, you need to have your profile updated with pictures and links to your website. Use the checklist in Appendix to make sure that you don't miss anything.

For authors, there are two sites that you should pay attention to your Amazon Author Central page and Goodreads.

Amazon Author Central[lxi]

Amazon offers authors a special profile page that you can update with information about yourself and your books. You can include pictures, videos, biography, blog post, and tour events. Once you have completed this page, when someone clicks your name on an Amazon book listing, they are taken to that page. If you don't have a website, make sure that you at least keep this page current.

GoodReads[lxii]

Goodreads is a social media platform that is for readers. It is the largest site for readers and book recommendations. Every author should have a presence on GoodReads not only as a reader but as an author. GoodReads has special features that will allow you as an author to connect with readers. There are also some groups that you can join that are organized by genre. This is great for interacting with real readers. If you write romance novels, you should be in romance novel groups to see what readers are saying about romance novels.

The Social Success Cycle

How do you get social media to work for you as an author? To be most successful on social media, you need to have a strategy in place. The strategy that I have found to be the most successful is known as the "Social Success Cycle." I don't know the origin of the term, but I was first introduced to it by Ryan Deiss and Russ Henneberry from Digital Marketer when I was studying for my Social and Community Manager certification. I found the concept to be fascinating because there were parts of it that I was already doing and found it to be rewarding. On the other hand, there were parts that I wasn't doing, and that explained why I wasn't having success in those areas.

The Social Success Cycle consists of four parts.

- Social Listening
- Social Influencing
- Social Networking
- Social Selling

Notice that social selling is the LAST step in the cycle. This is where a lot of people mess up. They start out trying to sell without listening, influencing or networking. You must date your audience.

Social Listening

It is my personal belief that social listening is the most important piece of the puzzle. If you are not listening, you are not able to respond properly. Think about this. If you put your fingers in your ears and closed your eyes and then tried to have a conversation with me, it would be a hot mess. You wouldn't be responding to what I was saying. You would be talking about what you wanted to talk about. If I then started talking about what you were talking about and asked you questions about it, you couldn't respond because you couldn't hear me. That is what it looks like when you post a bunch of stuff on Facebook, Twitter, Periscope, or LinkedIn and you haven't listened to your marketplace.

Traditionally, social listening is monitoring and responding to customer service and reputation management issues on social networks. It also includes listening and observing your target audience and finding out what issues they have that you can solve. Some people live their lives on social media. They post every thought they have. Does that irritate you? Does it get on your nerves? STOP IT! Never, ever say that again, particularly if you are a coach. I love to see people post about their problems with technology. Why? That means I don't have to guess what problems they are having, they are telling me.

That is why you need to be in groups that your target market is in. As an author, being in a group with other authors will not help you regarding sales. You need to be in the groups with people who would read your book.

This isn't just limited to social media. You should be listening wherever you are. If you are in an online class, listen to what people are talking about. Listen to their questions and concerns. Do they have problems that your company can provide a solution for?

I was recently part of a coaching class and was inspired to develop a service offering based on problems that students were having in the class. Dawniel Winningham teaches a fantastic course, LiveStream University, which shows you how to use platforms such as Periscope and Facebook Live, to promote your business. If you have ever seen her on livestream, you know that she is a beast when it comes to marketing on that platform. Well, she is also a beast when it comes to students in her class not having their homework.

The assignment involved the students doing their livestream on Periscope or Facebook Live daily. Well, that doesn't seem so hard, right? However, Dawniel has one rule of thumb; you don't go live without an offer. It can be an offer for a free report, or it can be to your core offer. It didn't matter. You needed to have a call to action that drove people to your landing page.

Well, that was the issue. Many people in the class did not have a landing page. They didn't have a website. They had products and services, but they had no way of completing those transactions (remember the "bottom line of business?"). These people needed landing pages.

I wish I could say that I was "listening" and responded appropriately on my own. I didn't. While I was accustomed to "social listening" while scrolling down my

Facebook feed or checking out LinkedIn groups, I missed this opportunity, initially. It took Dawniel, who is also my business coach, to literally say to me, "Vanessa, why don't you offer to do landing pages." After her telling me that a few times, I "listened." Listening added thousands to my bottom line.

Tips for Social Listening
Find 3 Facebook groups and 3 LinkedIn groups where your audience is and join them. Spend 5 minutes a day monitoring those groups. Get a notebook and jot down notes about what people are struggling with. Also, don't forget to listen to other online gatherings such as classes or webinars.

Social Influencing

To have a successful human dating relationship, you must show that you have something to bring to the table. You must show that you are a giving person. This is the phase of the relationship where you try to be as helpful as possible. Instead of going out to eat, you decide to cook a romantic dinner. For the gentleman, this may be where you offer to fix the leaky faucet because you want to show that you are helpful around the house.

Social Influencing on the web is very similar. It involves establishing authority on social networks through the distribution and sharing of valuable content. This is where you need your content marketing. You can dazzle your audience with your brilliance by creating valuable content. This is where you show that you have your finger on the pulse of your niche or industry because you are sharing the content of others that are respected in your field. You show you are an expert.

In my opinion, this is the most important part of the cycle. Yes, I know I said that about social listening. But if you just listen and never act, never create content and distribute it, never get on Periscope, never write your blog post, never do a Facebook Live...if you never do anything with that information that you heard, you are just a stalker. STOP IT. Take that information you jotted down during the social listening exercise and now develop some products and services. Do some Periscopes or write a blog post for the solution to a problem you heard. Share some information with your audience from someone else. Stop just "listening" and DO something.

Tips for Social Influencing
Find three real issues that your audience is having (use your social listening exercise). Develop a FREE digital product that solves a portion of that problem. You can write a blog post (if you don't have a blog, you can publish it on LinkedIn Pulse), do a series on Periscope or Facebook Live. You can record a video or an audio; it doesn't matter. Do something!

Social Networking
There are some powerful people who can help take your business to the next level, but they don't know who you are. Likewise, there are some great influencers in your industry that you don't know. It's time to change that.

Social Networking involves finding and associating with authoritative and influential people and brands on social networks. This is key to building your brand and audience. You must get in front of more people. The best way to do that is to have people put you in front of their audience. The best way to accomplish this is to put these people in front of your audience.

In my opinion, this is the most important part of the cycle. Yes, I know I said that about social listening and social influencing. But, if you just listen and never act; or if you listen, act and create content, but it never gets beyond your audience, your business will not grow. You must partner and collaborate with people to get your content in front of more people.

There are some powerful people who can help take your business to the next level, but they don't know who you are.

I have found that the best way to do this is by sharing other people's content with my audience. This has a ton of benefits. First, it allows me to share great content with my audience that I did not have to create. It allows me to share information about great upcoming events that my audience could be interested in. Listen, there is no room for competition. There is enough business to go around. When you show yourself friendly, you will be amazed at the business opportunities that become available.

This is how I landed one of my first "big" clients, Peak Performers Institute. The founders, Che Brown and Trevor Otts, are two of the greatest business minds of our time. I was asked to be a part of their team because of social networking, but I didn't know that was what I was doing at the time.

In February 2015, I had never heard of them. I received an email about an event that they were having called "72 Hours of Power." That virtual event was so life-changing for my business mindset that I was hooked. I started attending their Google Hangouts, and I participated in their virtual Facebook group. I started doing social networking, but I didn't know what that was at the time. I was just following directions. Trevor would say, "In the group, post your first name, your last name, where you are from and a little bit about your business." I did it.

He would ask us to post the nuggets in the Facebook group that we got from the session we were listening to. I did that but, I took it one step further. I had taken Sandi Krakowski's Twitter class, so I decided to open another browser and not only post those take-a-ways in the Facebook group, I decided to post them on Twitter where, in my mind, "other people would see it." Instead of putting the name of the person that had given the nugget, I would add their Twitter handle. It took a little extra work because I haven't heard of any of the people that were on the platform. So, I took the extra 30 seconds to look them up and grab their Twitter handles for the posts. It was worth it.

Guess what happen? When those speakers finished speaking, they would look at their Twitter account, and I would have blown up their notifications with what they had said. They loved it because it promoted them as a speaker and showed that someone was listening. They would retweet it and would follow me. Well, when others saw that Mr. or Mrs. Big Shot was retweeting my tweets, they would start following me as well. I ended up on Twitter lists for social media experts and small business gurus because I was sharing awesome content, even though it wasn't mine. Eventually, I got a call from Trevor Otts and Che Brown commending me for my engagement and asking me to be on their team. Those shares resulted in thousands of dollars of business for my company.

Tips for Social Networking
Find the 5 to 10 influencers in your industry and begin engaging with them online. Read and comment on their blogs. Share their events on Facebook and Twitter and make sure to tag them, if possible.

Social Selling
Finally, we get to the point where we can successfully make offers or tell people about your book. I am not saying to wait until you master the other three steps before you make offers. You need to be doing all of this

at the same time. However, you may not see great success with your offers until the first three items are clearly in motion.

Also, you want to make sure that you make the right offer to the right person at the right time in your relationship. You need a variety of things in your online superstore. You need free offers for people that don't know you. This could be blog posts, videos or content-rich social media posts. You need lead magnet offers that provide solutions to problems so that you are building your email list. Followers on your social media sites are worth zero until they get on your list. You need low priced products that you can offer to those that want to try you out. You need mid-range and high-end products as well.

In my opinion, this is the most important part of the cycle. Yes, I know I said that about social listening, social influencing, and social networking. But if you just listen and never act; or if you listen, act and create content, but it never gets beyond your audience; or you create content that goes viral, but you don't make the offer, you won't sell anything, and you won't make money. You can't pay your bills with likes and comments. You must convert your social media audience into buyers.

So, there it is, the Social Success Cycle. It starts with social listening, then social influencing, then social networking and finally social selling. But it doesn't end there. You must continue to listen, produce content, connect with influencers and make the sale.

20 Minute Social Success Cycle Power Plan

Sound overwhelming. It doesn't have to be. Here is a 20 minute a day Social Success Cycle Power Plan that will turn you into a profitable, online social butterfly in no time.

- Social Listening – Each day choose 1 Facebook or LinkedIn Group to monitor. Spend 5 minutes looking at the conversations and questions that were asked. Take notes.

- Social Influencing – When you find a problem that was asked that you could solve, spend 5 minutes outlining a solution. Schedule a time that you will complete the solution (blog post, video, audio, etc.).

- Social Networking – Use Twitter lists to organize key followers in your industry. Spend 5 minutes reviewing, responding and retweeting their comments.

- Social Selling – Make sure that you are posting about your book and other products and services at least a few times a week.

Chapter 11 - Email Marketing

*C*ontrary to popular belief, email marketing is far from dead. Many smart entrepreneurs use email marketing because it works. Consider these statistics:

- In 2017, global email users amounted to 3.7 billion users (Statista, 2019). This figure is set to grow to 4.3 billion users in 2022 (Statista, 2019).

- In 2017 alone, 269 billion emails were sent and received each day (Statista, 2019). This figure is expected to increase to over 333 billion daily emails in 2022 (Statista, 2019)

- For every $1 spent on emails marketing, you can expect an average return of $32 (DMA, 2018).

While there may be other communication vehicles that are getting attention, such as text message marketing, email is still important. Since email marketing isn't going anywhere anytime soon, let's look at the three types of emails you need in your business.

Types of Emails

Transactional

Transactional emails document the transactions that occur between you and your customers. It could be an email that provides a receipt for a purchase or an email that acknowledges that a class registration has been received. These emails are usually triggered in that something must happen (i.e., the purchase of an item) for the email to be sent.

Relational

These are emails that you send to engage with your audience and provide valuable content. This may be in the form of a newsletter or an email that is part of an automation campaign. These emails are usually sent in between promotional email campaigns.

Promotional

Promotional emails let your list know about products and services that you are offering. For many business owners, it seems as if these are the only emails they know how to send; the ones that say, "Buy my stuff."

Email Automation

Having a solid email marketing strategy is more than just having emails set up to be sent out on a schedule. Emails should be triggered not just by time, but by behavior. Your email marketing system should be able to send emails based on what your audience does or doesn't do.

A simple, timed based email strategy may look something like this:

- Immediately – Email sent when a person signs up for a lead magnet. (Transactional email)

- Day 1 – Follow up to lead magnet, offer additional valuable content. (Relational email)

- Day 3 – Email with additional content, maybe from a blog post. (Relational email)

- Day 5 – Email with more content and an offer to purchase the tripwire offer, which could be your book. (Promotional email)

- Day 7 - Email with more content (Relational email)

- Day 9 – Email with more content (Relational email)

- Day 11 – Email offering core offer, which could be the online class developed from your book. (Promotional email)

If you don't have any email strategy in place, the above schedule is a good place to start. However, it is far from what a real, automated strategy looks like. A real automated strategy looks at the behavior of the people receiving the email, and the next email is based on that behavior.

It may look something like this:

- Immediately – Email sent when a person signs up for a lead magnet. (Transactional email)

- o If email is opened and the link clicked, the person would proceed to the next email on the scheduled date.

- o If the email is opened, but the link is not clicked, the person would get an email reminding them to click the link to download the lead magnet.

- o If the email is not opened, the person is sent this email again perhaps with a different subject line.

- Day 1 – Follow up to lead magnet, offer additional valuable content. (Relational email)

  - o If email is opened, the person would proceed to the next email on the scheduled date.

  - o If the email is not opened, the person is sent this email again perhaps with a different subject line.

- Day 3 – Email with additional content, maybe from a blog post. (Relational email)

  - o If email is opened, the person would proceed to the next email on the scheduled date.

  - o If the email is not opened, the person is sent this email again perhaps with a different subject line.

- Day 5 – Email with more content and an offer to purchase your book. (Promotional email)

- o If email is opened and the link clicked, the person would proceed to the next email on the scheduled date.

- o If the email is opened, but the link is not clicked, the person would get another email telling them additional benefits from reading your book.

- o If the email is not opened, the person is sent this email again perhaps with a different subject line.

- Day 7 - Email with more content (Relational email)

  - o If email is opened, the person would proceed to the next email on the scheduled date.

  - o If the email is not opened, the person is sent this email again perhaps with a different subject line.

- Day 9 – Email with more content (Relational email)

  - o If email is opened, the person would proceed to the next email on the scheduled date.

  - o If the email is not opened, the person is sent this email again perhaps with a different subject line.

- Day 11 – Email offering core offer (your online class) (Promotional email)

- If email is opened, the person would proceed to the next email on the scheduled date.

- If the email is not opened, the person is sent this email again perhaps with a different subject line.

Most good email marketing solutions like GetResponse[lxiii], AWeber[lxiv] and Constant Contact[lxv] can handle this type of automation. It takes time to set something like this up, but it is worth it.

Segmentation

Email marketing is also an excellent way to segment your list. One way to use this strategy is to see what other products and services you offer that your audience may be interested in. Once you know what they are interested in, you can start engaging with them about that product solution.

An easy way to do this is to send an email to your list offering them a new lead magnet. The purpose of this is not to get their email address (you already have that) but to see what other items they are interested in.

Contrary to popular belief, email marketing is far from dead.

For instance, you may be a health and wellness coach. You have built your list based on content that deals specifically with nutrition and exercise. You are thinking about expanding your subject matter to cover weight loss. You would develop a lead magnet that you would not only use to grow your list but also to see who you currently have on your list that is interested in that subject. If your email marketing platform supports it, you could "tag" these people so that you market to them easily. Your initial email sequence may look something like this.

- Email to the entire list offering them the new lead magnet. It includes a link to a landing page with an opt-in form.

  o If the email is opened, link clicked, and form filled out; the person would be sent the transactional email that delivered the lead magnet and "tagged" in the system as a person that is highly interested.

  o If the email is opened, link clicked but form not filled out; the person would get an email reminding them to complete the form to get the free gift. The person is tagged as "interested."

  o If the email is opened, but the link is not clicked, the person is sent another email maybe worded differently.

  o If the email is not opened, the person is sent this email again perhaps with a different subject line or the person isn't sent anything at all because they are not interested in the subject matter.

Messenger Bots

Although we are talking email, I couldn't close this section without talking chatbot technology. Facebook Messenger Bots allow you to set up sequences similar to the ones described for emails in Facebook Messenger. You can provide content on a Facebook post that triggers a message in Messenger when someone responds on the post. You could then set up a similar nurture sequence where you provide valuable content. When they respond in Messenger, you have a 24-hour window where you can make a promotional offer. You can invite them to buy your book and sign up for another product/service such as your online class.

There are several bot platforms out there, but I have only used one, Manychat[lxvi], and I love it. If you are interested in learning more about creating a bots strategy, I suggest you check out my class, Bots Money Mastery. You will find it in my online store at MySmallBusinessLibrary.com[lxvii]. (Yeap, a shameless plug 😊.)

Chapter 12 – Developing Your #DigitalDynasty – Your 5 Figure Book Deal

*N*ow that you have all of this great information, it is time to implement. What does your product line look like for your book? Let's start putting some ideas on paper. Feel free to tweak and change as you see fit.

Book

Goal: Book Sales – Sell 100 books at $20 each

Strategy

- Make a list of 200 – 300 people who will buy your book. If this is your first book, don't forget to include family and friends. Many of them will support you because it is your first book, even if they are not your target audience. Reach out to them and let them know that your book is about to be released and make sure to invite them to your book signing.

- Take pre-orders online

- Reach out to those that you have a real relationship with on social media and let them know about your book.

Total expected: $2000

eBook

Goal: Sell $200 in Kindle Books and add 200 people to your mailing list

Strategy

- Price book at $0.99

- Do a series of livestreams to promote the book online

- Do a telesummit over a series of a few days where you invite ten speakers. Allow them to promote a free offer to build their list in exchange for giving away ten books. This will only cost them ten bucks.

- Make sure that you have a lead magnet in your Kindle version that will get people on your list. Workbooks, charts and other printables make great lead magnets for Kindle books because you can't include them in the actual eBook. Well, you can include them, but they look horrible.

- Sell 200 books

Total Expected: $200

Live Online Course Based on the Book

Goal: Develop an online class based on your book. Get 20 people in your class.

Example: 10-week class ($25 save your seat. $25/week for 10 weeks or $200 one-time payment)

Strategy

- Use Livestream, social media and email marketing to promote the class. Make sure to send emails to those who have purchased the book already

Total Expected - (If half pay $275 and half pay $200 = $4,750)

Video Product (Recording from Live Class)

Goal: Sell 20 units at $97

Strategy

- Develop lead magnets, blog posts and livestreams to talk about the issues that your class solves.

- Have participants write testimonials on how they enjoyed the class

- Do a webinar that teaches on one aspect that your class covers

- Use an email nurture sequence to provide valuable content and introduce your prospect to your offer.

- Run Facebook ads

Total Expected - $1,940

Conference or Live Event

Goal to have 50 attend your live event

Strategy

- Price ticket at $59

- Have ten vendor tables at $50 each

- Sell 20 books

- Offer from the stage - Sign up ten people for your 10-week coaching program ($49 a week for ten weeks)

- Manage your expenses. See if you can get sponsors for meals and snacks

Total expected: Event ($2950), Vendors ($500), Book sales ($400), Offer from Stage ($4900) = $8750

Recap

- Books - $2000
- eBooks - $200
- Online Course - $4750
- Video Product - $1940
- Conference/Live Event - $8750

Total Revenue: $17,640

Of course, you can add and subtract from this. If you don't want to do a live event, you can add a membership program or one-on-one coaching. The idea is to plan this ahead of time so that you know where you are going as you launch your book.

Chapter 13 – Pulling It All Together

*W*e made it to the end! Woo Hoo! Believe it or not, we have only scratched the surface. There are so many things you can do with your book, but I am sure that this is enough to get you started. Yes, the party is JUST STARTING.

Next Steps

What is the very next thing you should do? Visit ChiefExecutiveAuthor.com[lxviii] and make sure that you have downloaded the worksheets that go along with the book. Also, look at the free training videos on the resource page. They may answer some of the questions that you have. Also, make sure that you join our free, private Facebook Group – Digital Mastery for Authors[lxix]. Here you can ask your questions and network with other CEAs.

If you would like to learn more about how to implement the principles outlined in this book, I would love the opportunity to work with you. Visit our websites Digital Mastery Academy[lxx] or Chief Executive Author[lxxi] to learn about our upcoming courses and coaching programs.

I appreciate you purchasing this book. If you have time, please leave a review on Amazon. I hope that you have found this book to be helpful. Please reach out to me if I can assist you with your book writing, publishing or digital marketing needs. You can schedule your free consultation at <u>TalkWithVan.com</u>[lxxii].

Appendices

Appendix 1 – Online Resources for Writers

These links were all good as of April 2019. ☺

Brainstorming

MindMapping[lxxiii]

Mind mapping is an excellent way to brainstorm and organize ideas. This site provides great insight to those that are new to the process. It also includes information on some of the computer software and applications available.

Coggle[lxxiv]

Coggle is a free, simple to use mind mapping tool that allows online collaboration. You can save your mind map as a PDF or PNG.

Research

Feedly[lxxv]

Feedly is a news aggregator application for various web browsers and mobile devices. It compiles news feeds from a variety of online sources based on your choices. You can then save those articles to various "read later" applications like Pocket and Instapaper.

InfoPlease[lxxvi]

InfoPlease combines an encyclopedia, almanac, dictionary, thesaurus, atlas, and biography reference.

FedStats[lxxvii]

This site gives access to statistics from more than 100 government agencies.

U.S. Census Bureau[lxxviii]

This site provides data from the Census Bureau online.

Wikipedia[lxxix]

Wikipedia is a multilingual, web-based, free-content encyclopedia written collaboratively by mostly anonymous internet volunteers. Since anyone can edit the articles, you shouldn't use it as your sole source of information. However, it can be a great way to get basic information and find out where to look for additional references.

Instapaper[lxxx]

Instapaper is a cloud-based tool that allows you to save web articles for later reading. You can then access them on any of your mobile devices.

Pocket[lxxxi]

Pocket is also a "read later" tool that allows you to file articles you come across in your internet research. It has a few other features, including the ability to save embedded video from articles. You can also send articles to other people via email or directly to other Pocket users.

Evernote[lxxxii]

Evernote is a research organization tool that allows you to capture and store your notes, web clips, files, and images. You can access them anytime from your computer or another mobile device.

Creative Commons[lxxxiii]

Creative Commons allows you to give the public permission to share and use your creative work if they give you credit. Creative Commons' licenses work in conjunction with your standard copyright and enable you to modify your copyright terms to best suit your needs.

Write

Open Office[lxxxiv]

Open Office is free, open source software which includes a word processor, presentation and spreadsheet program.

Google Drive[lxxxv]

Google Drive (previously known as Google Docs) is a cloud-based application that allows you to store and create documents, spreadsheets, presentations, forms, and drawings. You can share, collaborate and sync your documents also.

ZohoDocs[lxxxvi]

Zoho is another free word processing suite, like Google Drive. It allows desktop syncing, file sharing, word processing and includes a spreadsheet and presentation tool.

Scrivener[lxxxvii]

Scrivener is a word processor and project management tool that allows you to outline and structure your ideas, take notes and view research alongside your writing. It is great for writing novels, articles, short stories, and screenplays. They offer a free trial.

Zamzar[lxxxviii]

Zamzar is a free, online converter that allows you to convert documents, images, music, and video. They support over 1200 file types. It is a great tool to convert word processing documents to pdf, epub or other required formats.

Edit

APA Style[lxxxix]

This blog gives you access to the fundamentals of the American Psychological Association (APA) style.

The Chicago Manual of Style Online[xc]

This is the online resource for the popular Chicago Manual of Style. This site includes an online forum and basic style rules.

The Elements of Style[xci]

This site is based on the classic book by Strunk and White.

Dictionary.com[xcii]

Dictionary.com is the world's leading, online resource for everything word related. The site includes definitions, synonyms, audio pronunciations, example sentences, translations and spelling help through their partner services Thesaurus.com and Reference.com.

Acronym Finder[xciii]

Acronym Finder is the world's largest dictionary of acronyms, abbreviations, and initialisms. When used in conjunction with the Acronym Attic, Acronym Finder contains more than 5 million acronyms and abbreviations.

RhymeZone[xciv]

Find rhymes, near rhymes, homophones, synonyms and definitions for a given word.

Grammar Girl[xcv]

Grammar Girl is an excellent source for information on proper word usage and punctuation.

Grammar Handbook[xcvi]

The Center for Writing Studies at the University of Illinois Champaign-Urbana offers access to this grammar handbook which includes basic grammar rules, citation styles, and writing tips.

Easybib.com[xcvii]

Easybib.com is an online tool that will generate a "Works Cited" page instantly in Modern Language Association (MLA) style for free. Over 59 other styles, including APA and Chicago, are included in their membership.

Store

OneDrive[xcviii]

OneDrive is a Microsoft product that allows you to store and access your files on your desktop, tablet or smartphone. OneDrive also works with several applications including Easybib.

Dropbox[xcix]

Dropbox allows you to store, share and access your documents online from anywhere you have an internet connection, including your phone or mobile device.

Resources listed here will help you register and publish your paperback, hardback or eBook.

Publish

Amazon's Kindle Direct Publishing[c]

Amazon's Kindle Direct Publishing (KDP) allows you to publish your books independently to the Amazon Kindle Store. The service allows global distribution and the ability to publish in multiple languages including English, German, French, Spanish, Portuguese, Italian, and Japanese.

Lulu[ci]

Lulu is a print on demand service that allows you to print and distribute paperback, hardback, and eBooks.

Ingram Sparks[cii]

Ingram Sparks is a print on demand service that allows you to print and distribute paperback, hardback, and eBooks.

Smashwords[ciii]

Smashwords is an eBook self-publishing and distribution platform.

U.S. Copyright Office[civ]
The US Copyright Office allows you the additional protection of your written work for a fee.

Library of Congress[cv]
The Library of Congress catalog control number is a unique identification number assigned to books that will be submitted to the Library of Congress. The Preassigned Control Number (PCN) program is to enable the Library of Congress to assign control numbers in advance of publication.

Resources listed here will help you get the word out about your work.

Promote

Goodreads[cvi]
Goodreads is the world's largest site for readers and book recommendations with over 25 million members.

BookTalk[cvii]
Book Talk is a free book discussion group with thousands of members. Members read and discuss fiction, non-fiction, short stories, and poetry and host live chats and interviews with authors.

BookBuzzr[cviii]
BookBuzzr offers a do it yourself online book marketing technology suite. The BookBuzzr widget is a portable book website with a flipping pages feature allowing you to invite your readers to sample your book.

PR Log[cix]

PR Log is an online press release distribution and press release submission service. They offer free and premium service packages.

Free Press Release[cx]

Free-press-release.com (FPR) provides feed and premium press release distribution services.

Sell

PayPal[cxi]

PayPal allows you to accept all forms of payments anywhere you do business. Many online customers prefer PayPal because their financial data, such as credit card numbers, is not shared with the merchant. The PayPal Here app for your smartphone will allow you to accept credit cards and checks.

Square Up[cxii]

The Square is a device that allows you to accept credit cards using your smartphone. You can also track checks and gift certificates, but no funds are actually transferred. Transactions from Square are transferred to your bank account the next day.

Flint[cxiii]

Flint is an app that allows you to accept credit cards from your smartphone without a card reader. It includes mobile invoicing and digital coupons. Deposits are made in one to two days.

WooCommerce[cxiv]

WooCommerce is a popular WordPress eCommerce plugin. This free toolkit allows you to set up an online store on your self-hosted WordPress Blog.

Ecwid[cxv]

Ecwid is an eCommerce shopping cart that allows you to set up an online store within your Facebook fan page or self-hosted WordPress site.

Appendix 2 – Social Media Checklist for Authors

Social media is a tool to use to help you meet your business goals. The key to sales on social media is engagement. You should be active on at least 2 of the following social media platforms in addition to having your Amazon Author Central page completed. Use the following checklist to make sure that you complete your profiles of the given platforms.

Amazon Author Central page
(https://authorcentral.amazon.com/)
- [ ] Bio
- [ ] Photos
- [ ] Video
- [ ] Blog
- [ ] Twitter Feed
- [ ] Events

Facebook Business Page
- [ ] Profile image
- [ ] Cover image
- [ ] Call to action (Should lead to where they can buy your book)

Goodreads
(https://www.goodreads.com/)
- [ ] Join the Goodreads Author Program
- [ ] Profile image
- [ ] Blogs
- [ ] Events

Twitter (You don't need a separate account for your book)

- ☐ Profile image
- ☐ Cover image
- ☐ Bio (Include a few hashtags)

Periscope (Connect with Twitter account)

- ☐ Profile image
- ☐ Cover image
- ☐ Bio

LinkedIn

- ☐ Profile Image
- ☐ Cover Image
- ☐ Profile (Make sure to include your publications)

Instagram

- ☐ Profile image
- ☐ Bio (Make sure link to website is in bio.)
- ☐ Use a recipe from IFTTT to post to native pictures to Twitter

Pinterest

- ☐ Profile image
- ☐ Bio
- ☐ Have at least one board dedicated to your books

Appendix 3 - Endnotes

Chapter 1

[i] Lin, Tom C. W. (April 23, 2014). "CEOs and Presidents". Retrieved June 29, 2017 – via papers.SSRN.com.

Chapter 2

[ii] https://www.facebook.com/groups/digitalmasteryforauthors/

Chapter 4

[iii] https://www.fiverr.com/

Chapter 5

[iv] "It Takes 6 to 8 Touches to Generate a Viable Sales Lead. Here's Why." Salesforce Blog, www.salesforce.com/blog/2015/04/takes-6-8-touches-generate-viable-sales-lead-heres-why-gp.html.

[v] www.Paypal.com

[vi] www.squareup.com

Chapter 6

[vii] https://www.amazon.com/dp/B007URVZJ6

[viii] https://sourceforge.net/projects/audacity

[ix] http://www.acx.com

[x] https://easydigitaldownloads.com/

[xi] https://sellfy.com

[xii] https://aws.amazon.com/s3/

[xiii] https://wistia.com/

[xiv] https://iplayerhd.com/

[xv] https://www.techsmith.com/video-editor.html

[xvi] https://zoom.us/

[xvii] https://moodle.org

[xviii] https://www.udemy.com

xix www.FreeConferenceCalling.com

xx https://www.freeconferencecallhd.com/us-en/

xxi https://www.uberconference.com/

xxii https://soundcloud.com/

xxiii https://audioboom.com/

xxiv https://www.toastmasters.org

xxv https://www.learndash.com/

xxvi https://www.tipsandtricks-hq.com/wordpress-emember-easy-to-use-wordpress-membership-plugin-1706

xxvii https://memberpress.com/

xxviii https://www.paidmembershipspro.com/

xxix https://member.wishlistproducts.com/

xxx https://www.memberclicks.com/

xxxi https://www.canva.com/

xxxii https://www.getresponse.com/

xxxiii https://www.timetrade.com

xxxiv https://acuityscheduling.com/

xxxv https://calendly.com/

xxxvi https://www.paypal.com/us/home

xxxvii https://stripe.com

xxxviii https://squareup.com/us/en

xxxix https://www.moonclerk.com/

xl https://www.uberconference.com/

xli https://www.zoom.us/

xlii https://www.startapp.com/

xliii https://www.upwork.com/

xliv https://www.appypie.com/

xlv https://www.appmakr.com/

Chapter 7

xlvi https://www.ama.org/AboutAMA/Pages/Definition-of-marketing.aspx

Chapter 8

xlvii https://business.linkedin.com/marketing-solutions/blog/best-practices--content-marketing/2016/what-is-content-marketing--definitions-from-25-thought-leaders

xlviii https://www.wordstream.com/blog/ws/2017/03/08/video-marketing-statistics

Chapter 9

xlix https://www.facebook.com/business/learn/facebook-ads-basics

l
https://www.facebook.com/business/help/976240832426180?helpref=faq_content

li https://business.linkedin.com/marketing-solutions/ads

lii https://ads.twitter.com/login

liii https://www.google.com/ads

liv https://www.youtube.com/yt/advertise/

lv https://ads.pinterest.com/

lvi https://forbusiness.snapchat.com/

lvii https://secure.bingads.microsoft.com/

lviii https://gemini.yahoo.com/advertiser/home

lix http://cdn2.hubspot.net/hub/18316/file-13370555-pdf/docs/customer-avatar-workbook.pdf

Chapter 10

[lx] https://www.statista.com/statistics/272014/global-social-networks-ranked-by-number-of-users/

[lxi] https://authorcentral.amazon.com/

[lxii] https://www.goodreads.com/

Chapter 11

[lxiii] https://www.getresponse.com/

[lxiv] https://www.aweber.com/home.htm

[lxv] https://www.constantcontact.com/index.jsp

[lxvi] https://manychat.com

[lxvii] http://mysmallbusinesslibrary.com/

Chapter 13

[lxviii] ChiefExecutiveAuthor.com

[lxix] https://www.facebook.com/groups/digitalmasteryforauthors/

[lxx] DigitalMasteryAcademy.com

[lxxi] ChiefExecutiveAuthor.com

[lxxii] TalkWithVan.com

[lxxiii] https://www.mindmapping.com/

[lxxiv] https://coggle.it/

[lxxv] http://feedly.com/

[lxxvi] http://www.infoplease.com/

[lxxvii] http://www.fedstats.gov/

[lxxviii] http://www.census.gov/

[lxxix] http://www.wikipedia.org/

[lxxx] http://www.instapaper.com/

[lxxxi] http://getpocket.com/

lxxxii http://evernote.com/

lxxxiii http://creativecommons.org/

lxxxiv http://www.openoffice.org/

lxxxv https://drive.google.com/

lxxxvi https://www.zoho.com/

lxxxvii https://www.literatureandlatte.com/scrivener/overview

lxxxviii http://www.zamzar.com/

lxxxix http://www.apastyle.org/

xc http://www.chicagomanualofstyle.org/home.html

xci http://www.bartleby.com/141/index.html

xcii http://dictionary.reference.com/

xciii http://www.acronymfinder.com/

xciv http://www.rhymezone.com/

xcv http://www.quickanddirtytips.com/grammar-girl

xcvi http://www.cws.illinois.edu/workshop/writers/

xcvii http://www.easybib.com/

xcviii https://onedrive.live.com/

xcix https://www.dropbox.com/

c https://kdp.amazon.com/

ci http://www.lulu.com/

cii https://www.ingramspark.com/

ciii https://www.smashwords.com/

civ http://www.copyright.gov/

cv http://www.loc.gov/publish/pcn/

cvi https://www.goodreads.com/

cvii http://booktalk.org/

[cviii] http://www.bookbuzzr.com/

[cix] http://www.prlog.org/

[cx] http://www.free-press-release.com/

[cxi] https://www.paypal.com/

[cxii] https://squareup.com/

[cxiii] https://www.flint.com/

[cxiv] http://www.woothemes.com/woocommerce/

[cxv] http://www.ecwid.com/